The Civilization of the American Indian Series

The Osage Ceremonial Dance
I'n-Lon-Schka

The Osage Ceremonial Dance I'n-Lon-Schka

By Alice Anne Callahan

University of Oklahoma Press : Norman and London

Dedicated to the memory of my father, Charles Callahan, an original Osage allottee.

Photographs on pages 36, 39, 67, 68, 110, and 117 are by Jack E. Looney; on pages 26, 47, 114, 123, and 132, by Alice Anne Callahan; on pages 10, 11, 48, and 54 by Jean Cox; on pages 23 and 30, from the Osage Tribal Museum, Pawhuska; on page 42, by Don Creighton.

Library of Congress Cataloging-in-Publication Data

Callahan, Alice Anne, 1926–
    The osage ceremonial dance I'n-Lon-schka / Alice Anne Callahan.
        p.   cm. — (The Civilization of the American Indian series)
    Includes bibliographical references.
    ISBN 0-8061-2284-6 (alk. paper)
    1. Osage Indians—Dances.   2. Osage Indians—Rites and
ceremonies.
    I. Title.   II. Series.
    E99.O8C35   1990
    394'.3—dc20   90-50230
                                                                        CIP

The paper in this book meets the guidelines for permanence and durability of the Committee on Production Guidelines for Book Longevity of the Council on Library Resources, Inc. ∞

The Osage Ceremonial Dance I'n-Lon-Schka is Volume 201 in The Civilization of the American Indian Series.

Contents

Preface   xi
Acknowledgments   xvii
Introduction   3
Chapters
    1. Cultural and Historical Beginnings   7
    2. The History of the I'n-Lon-Schka   19
    3. Traditions of the I'n-Lon-Schka   33
    4. The I'n-Lon-Schka Music   73
    5. The I'n-Lon-Schka Dance   97
    6. The Osage Traditional Dress   108
    7. New Ways for Old Traditions   127
    8. Significance of the I'n-Lon-Schka   135
Appendix
    A. Grayhorse District 1974–75 I'n-Lon-Schka
       Organization   141
    B. Gifts Presented at the Acceptance-of-the-Drum
       Ceremony   143
    C. Individual and Family Songs   145
Notes   147
Bibliography   157
Index   163

Illustrations

Figures
1. White Hair (Pah-Hu-Skah), head chief
   of the Osages 9
2. Osage Agency at Pawhuska, Oklahoma 10
3. Osage landscape near Burbank, Oklahoma ... 11
4. Early Osage I'n-Lon-Schka dancers 23
5. Archie Mason, with traditional headdress 26
6. Grayhorse Community roundhouse, 1912 30
7. The new 1975 Grayhorse Drumkeeper,
   Curtis Oren Bear 36
8. The dance chairmen at Grayhorse, Hominy,
   and Pawhuska, 1974 39
9. Jerry Shaw, a Grayhorse Whipman 42
10. The I'n-Lon-Schka drum being brought in
    by the Drum Warmer and his assistant 45
11. Osage Head Singer Morris Lookout 47
12. The singers' circle at Grayhorse 48
13. A spectator at Grayhorse 54
14. Diagram of the traditional seating positions . 58
15. Introduction-to-the-Dance Ceremony for
    a young man 67
16. Introduction-to-the-Dance Ceremony for
    a young boy 68
17. Typical upright position used by the men
    dancers in the I'n-Lon-Schka 101
18. "Going-down" position used by the men
    dancers in the I'n-Lon-Schka 102
19. Positions of the dancers in the I'n-Lon-Schka 103
20. Correct toe-heel position 104
21. Crossed toe-heel step 105
22. Typical arm positions in I'n-Lon-Schka dancing 106

23. Examples of Osage men's traditional dress 110
24. Georgeann Robinson in Osage women's
    traditional dress 114
25. An Osage moccasin 116
26. Osage bridal dress 117
27. Osage ribbon-work designs of horse,
    diamonds, and arrow 120
28. Osage ribbon-work designs of prong
    and diamond 121
29. Osage ribbon-work designs of hands
    and small diamonds 121
30. Osage ribbon-work designs of small diamonds 122
31. Maudie Cheshewalla demonstrating finger
    weaving 123
32. Double-chevron finger-weaving design 124
33. Double-diamond finger-weaving design 125
34. Ed Red Eagle, Sr., at the 1987 Pawhuska
    I'n-Lon-Schka 132

Maps
1. Lands Ceded by the Osages, 1808–1870 8
2. Indian Tribes of Oklahoma 23
3. Map of Osage County, Oklahoma 24

Music Examples
1. Common intervals found in American
   Indian melodies 75
2. Franklin Shaw Individual Song 80
3. Range of the Franklin Shaw Individual Song 81
4. Beginning Song at Grayhorse, Hominy,
   and Pawhuska 81
5. Range of the Beginning Song 81
6. Hunk-A-Hoppy Individual Song (excerpt) 82
7. Thomas Joe Lane Individual Song (excerpt) 83
8. A 1914 Osage Song's melodic rhythm patterns 86
9. A 1914 Osage song's melodic rhythm patterns 86
10. Franklin Shaw Individual Song's melodic
    rhythm patterns 87
11. Beginning Song's melodic rhythm patterns 87
12. Trot Song's melodic rhythm patterns 87

Preface

Whereas, Alice Anne Callahan, an adult unallotted member of the Osage Tribe of Indians, is of less than one-half Indian blood,

Now, therefore, pursuant to Part 123.5, Title 25, Code of Federal Regulations, and in compliance with the act of Feb. 5, 1948 (62 Stat. 18) the Superintendent of the Osage Agency does hereby issue to the said . . . Alice Anne Callahan . . . this Certificate of Competency.

Done at Pawhuska, Oklahoma, this 20th day of March, 1948. . . .[1]

My family link to the Osage Indians stems from one Osage woman, Mary Louise Tayrien, my great-great-grandmother. Mary Louise Tayrien married A. B. Canville, a French-Canadian Indian trader and close associate of the famed Chouteau trading family.[2] A. B. Canville built the first permanent home of a white settler in what is now Neosho County, Kansas, in 1844—the Canville Trading Post. He chose high ground for the trading post overlooking the Neosho River at the ford which later carried his name. One historian of the area has found that "all Indian trails led straight across the country, ending at the crossing at Canville Ford, the earliest ford of any record across the Neosho River."[3]

The Canville Trading Post's chief distinction was that it was the site of negotiations leading to the Osage treaty of 1865, in which the Osages ceded the territory that now comprises Neosho and Labette counties in Kansas to the United States. A historical marker at Shaw, Kansas, in Neosho County near the Neosho River, bears the following inscription: "In 1844 A. B. Canville established a Trading Post among the Osages a little Southeast of this marker. Here on Sept. 29, 1865, the Osages signed a treaty with the Federal Government agreeing to a reduction of their Reserve in Kansas. A few years later they were removed to Oklahoma."[4]

Throughout our lives my sisters and I have been aware and proud of our Osage heritage and have shared the interest and love for the Osage of our father, Charles Callahan (deceased since December, 1987). This pride in my Osage heritage shaped my choice of the I'n-Lon-Schka as a topic for study. As the I'n-Lon-Schka is the most important surviving ceremonial Osage dance, and as it has not been described in any of the published Osage histories or social scientific studies, it has been my aim to examine, describe, interpret insofar as is possible, and understand the I'n-Lon-Schka in Osage terms, emphasizing the arts of music, dance, and costume. By recording what has not been previously recorded, this study may aid in the preservation of a significant tribal ceremony.

Since the 1880s, when the Osages received the I'n-Lon-Schka, the Osages have handed down orally from one generation to the next the music, dance, and traditions of this ceremony. Therefore, I have depended heavily on interviews with persons who have had close knowledge of the I'n-Lon-Schka and who were willing to spend time talking with me. Oral sources were an indispensable part of my study. As much of the information from these persons is overlapping, it has not always been possible to attribute specific information to each person individually. Therefore, the information on the I'n-Lon-Schka is my interpretation of conversations with these oral sources, combined with my own research. Receiving the help, support, and cooperation of John Joseph Mathews, Osage author and historian; former Grayhorse Dance Chairman and advisor Archie Mason; Ed Red Eagle, Pawhuska Dance Chairman and assistant chief of the Osage Nation during my years of research; Morris Lookout, Head Singer during my years of research; and Maudie Cheshewalla, Osage museum curator during my years of research, were crucial to the success and completion of this study. Personally sharing a cultural and blood relation enabled me to talk to family and other tribal members who might otherwise have been unavailable and to have access to materials in such private collections as that of the Shaw family. My father's library of Osage history and the interviews I recorded with John Joseph Mathews have been enormously helpful.

During the winter of 1975 I spent the month of January in Pawhuska, Oklahoma, studying the Osage language with Mabel Logan. Although there is an Osage dictionary written by Francis La Flesche, I wanted to study the language by way of the Osage oral tradition. I made tapes of the language and wrote out cards with the Osage words and expressions described phonetically. This competency in the Osage language aided me in the recognition and discussion of specialized terms in the interviews.

Of course, there have been difficulties in gathering information from oral sources. Among these has been my own inexperience in field work. Long practice was required before I learned what questions to ask; to piece together fragments of information; to listen for leads to missing information; to evaluate contrasting, differing, and contradictory information; to recognize and respect information that was secret or too personal to be included. On occasion I encountered reluctance, suspicion, and hostility from some tribal members who felt that the I'n-Lon-Schka should remain strictly an oral tradition and should be neither recorded nor written down. I have been privileged to learn as much as I have because I have been sympathetic with the beliefs of the tribe, because I have chosen not to record information when I believed it would be harmful to the I'n-Lon-Schka to do so, and because I have rigorously reviewed my observations and interpretations with several respected Osages who have had a long, intimate association with the ceremonies.

My procedures for gathering the information from oral sources involved taping and taking notes during interviews; comparing and contrasting the information I received from several oral sources; matching the information from oral sources with my own observations at the I'n-Lon-Schkas held in Hominy, Pawhuska, and Grayhorse during the summers of 1974 through 1987; reinterviewing former oral sources or interviewing new ones when the information was conflicting or incomplete; and rechecking the information on return trips to Oklahoma during the years in which I collected information.

During the 1980s I revisited my former oral sources—Ed

Red Eagle, Archie Mason, Morris Lookout, and Maudie Cheshewalla—to give them an opportunity to make additions or cor-
rections to the original manuscript. I also consulted some new
oral sources—primarily Archie Mason, Jr., and Ed Red Eagle, Jr.

I have made a very deliberate effort to report what I have
learned honestly, without distortion, and without exploiting either my privileged information or the Osage Tribe. I have tried
to remain sensitive to the cultural differences that are necessarily a part of any study of this sort, and I have not included
information that I thought would invade or compromise either
tribal privacy or the tribal sense of sacred propriety. Drafts of
information credited to my oral sources were shown to them to
read, correct, augment, approve, or disapprove before I shared
the information with my readers at Syracuse University, where
I wrote a dissertation on the I'n-Lon-Schka for my doctorate in
humanities in 1977.

For this study I have made a comprehensive documentary
record of the I'n-Lon-Schka ceremonies by means of still photographs and tapes of the actual dance ceremonies as they oc-
curred. The difficulties encountered in both taping and photographing were plentiful. Sound recording was not allowed at
some of the I'n-Lon-Schka dances; when it was allowed, the
mixture of crowd sounds, bells, and drumbeats made it very difficult to obtain clearly defined recordings of melodies, rhythms,
and words with the portable equipment that I was able to use.
Likewise, photography was not allowed at all in some of the
I'n-Lon-Schka dances, and only at certain times in other of
the dances, and the lighting within the dance arbor made it very
difficult to take good, clear, useful pictures. Further, the policies
governing taping and photographing changed from year to year
according to the views of the different Drumkeepers and Dance
Chairmen; the changes were not made by whim, but by careful
consideration of a difficult issue. Modern technology and modern scholarship as well are, after all, intrusions into sacred, cher-
ished traditions. Each year I had to determine the new policies
for taping and photographing; sometimes I had to learn them
the hard way, as when I traveled to Oklahoma with a photographer only to learn that the dance organization had set a policy
of no photography whatever during the dances.

In some instances my original plans had to be modified or abandoned, as with my original intent to transcribe the I'n-Lon-Schka song texts, which remained elusive and essentially untranslatable for me. Some of the songs belong to individuals and families and as strictly private songs are not available for discussion, and it was impossible for me to record or otherwise obtain other texts.

I have no illusion that my study represents the final word on the subject, as the ceremonial tradition will undoubtedly continue to be modified with the passage of time. I understand that no book can record completely what this dance means to the Osage tribe or to Osages individually. However, as a writer I am taking down the images of what my oral sources saw "in the mirror." There will always be some who say, "That's not my image," but the writer's duty is to record and interpret according to her own understanding.

ALICE ANNE CALLAHAN

Acknowledgments

W ell aware that I am indebted to a very large number of people for their help and support during my work on this study of the I'n-Lon-Schka, I nonetheless would particularly like to express my thanks to the following: My father, Charles Callahan, for his sharing of his knowledge and materials on Osage history, his continuing interest and support in this study, and his patience and humor as my sounding board; Professor David Tatham of Syracuse University, my dissertation advisor, for making the distance between Kansas and New York not impossible through his welcome response to my phone calls and through his many detailed letters criticizing my writing and offering good advice and encouragement at different stages of this work; John Joseph Mathews, for giving me some much needed help and advice in the very early stages of my field work, and directing me to people to interview and for authoritative information on Osage history.

Very special thanks go to those persons who served as my oral sources throughout the 1970s and 1980s for their patience and willingness to spend long hours answering my questions and reading my materials—in particular, Archie Mason and Ed Red Eagle for their information on I'n-Lon-Schka history and traditions; Morris Lookout for his important information on I'n-Lon-Schka music, musicians, and traditions; Maudie Cheshewalla, Georgeann Robinson, and Ida Penn for their information on Osage ribbon work, finger weaving, traditional dress and I'n-Lon-Schka traditions.

I also thank Mrs. Julia Mason for materials on her grandfather, James Bigheart; Mabel Logan for her assistance with the Osage language; Jean Cox and Jack Looney for their expert help in photography; Syracuse University Professors William Fleming and Abraham Veinus for encouraging me in the initial stages of selecting a dissertation topic and for giving me good advice on methods and procedures to use in my work; Professors Frank Macomber, Barry Glassner, and William Fleming for reading my manuscript and making helpful suggestions during the revisions; and Professor Carol Talbott, whose early comments on chapter 3 made me more confident of my field work.

Thanks go to John Shaw, who shared with me his experiences as a former member of the Grayhorse Dance Committee as well as information on the Shaw family; to my husband, Tom Russell, for his steady support and help through the revisions of the 1980s and for his and my niece Christine Musgrave's sketches and line drawings which replaced my poor efforts; to my sister Mary Jane Chubb for suggesting to me that I write on the I'n-Lon-Schka; to my sister Charlene Potter for her drawings of the Osage finger weaving and ribbon work designs; to my Hessert aunts in Chautauqua, Kansas, who supplied a way-station for me; to friends and family who accompanied me on the long trips to Oklahoma; to the many Tulsa, Pawhuska, Burbank, and Grayhorse, Oklahoma, residents who offered their hospitality and assistance; to all of my family for being patient with my "hibernations"; to Loda Newcomb for typing the final dissertation copy; to Phyllis Braun, who helped in putting the revised manuscript on a word processor; and to Professor Terry P. Wilson, University of California, Berkeley, who read the revised manuscript and offered suggestions pertaining to style and content.

The Osage Ceremonial Dance
I'n-Lon-Schka

Introduction

The importance of the dance in the life of the Indian is shown in the fact that his most elaborate religious ceremonies are commonly known as dances.[1]

Authorities are agreed that dance ceremonies in the tribal societies of the world—whether in Africa, Asia, or America—are both sacred and secular in nature. They were used to achieve specific results, such as success in war and the hunt, the treatment and curing of the sick, protection from evil, and the fertility of crops and animals, and as a means of communicating with the Great or Guardian Spirit. They were also used to designate status, to transmit values and norms to tribal members, and to maintain the solidarity of a tribe. Through dance and music and prayers the mysterious forces of nature and the supernatural were brought under control. An Indian said, "If a man is to do something more than human, he must have more than human power." The dance ceremonies were essential to obtain that "more than human power." Since both music and dance were believed to be endowed with mystical powers, they were much more important in the lives of Indians and persons of other tribal societies than they were in the lives of Europeans. Because of this close relationship between music, dance, and religion in the world's tribal cultures, the musicologist Siegrid Nadel formulated a theory that music and dance ceremonies must have begun as a special means by which human beings communicated with the supernatural.[2]

Dance ceremonies reflect and symbolize for tribal peoples the very ethos of their lives. When the Bantus of Africa asked a stranger what he or she danced, they believed that from the response they learned all that was essential about the stranger's people. Nothing depicts the essence of an American Indian

3

more eloquently than his or her dance ceremonies, which reveal all that is characteristic of the individual's tribe—their attitude toward life, their relationship to nature, their faith, their convictions, their joys and sorrows.[3]

There are some common characteristics among the dance ceremonies of all North American Indian tribes, and these seem to have persisted for many generations. Most ceremonials consist of two parts, one private, limited to the dancers, and one public, in the sense that other, nondancing members of the tribe attend. Usually the first part of the ceremonial is a private retreat for the dancing participants, while the second, public part has as its most important feature the dance proper. The degrees of secrecy in the dances vary from tribe to tribe, with each group making its own decisions about what constitutes the public and private portions of the ceremony. The dance steps and movements are generally dignified and restrained, and the dancers are always appropriately costumed in the traditional dress of the tribe.[4]

The powwow, which differs from the sacred dances in being more of a social event and secular ceremony, has been and continues to be an important part of the life of all American Indians. It is now primarily a social coming together, a sharing and reaffirming of old ways in a secular fashion. An Osage Head Singer, Morris Lookout, in reflecting on dance ceremonies, said that they indicated to him a spiritually oriented dance in a spiritual background or setting. By contrast, the powwow dance was a socially oriented dance in a secular setting and festive atmosphere. Even though the distinction is not as clear today as it was in the past, the emphasis in the powwow remains social rather than religious.[5]

As the powwows are primarily for entertainment and usually festive dances of celebration, they are often participated in for the sheer joy of dancing. This experience is out of place in ceremonial dancing, in which the dance stops if in its course it "gets good." The dancers will then be ready to come back for more the next day or the next year.[6] In the powwow, the dance sometimes continues all night "if the dancing gets good."

The American colonialists and missionaries not only tried to push the Indians from their lands, but they also tried to eradicate Indian culture. This lack of sympathy for others' culture was reflected in the outlawing of many of the Indian ceremonial dances by the close of the nineteenth century—especially the Ghost Dance and the Sun Dance. Indian agents in South Dakota in the 1880s referred to the Sun Dance as that "heathenish annual ceremony . . . and that aboriginal and barbarous festival." Through the influence of missionaries, Indian agents, and other white interest groups against these "pagan" ceremonies, the Interior Department formulated a criminal code in the late nineteenth century forbidding Indian religious practices. Penalties were established, and this criminal code was in effect till 1933. These laws of the whites served the purpose of decreasing the threat (to the whites) of the collective solidarity of the tribes.[7]

It is only because of the importance of these dances in the Indians' lives and their determination to keep them that any have survived today. These dance ceremonies, such as the I'n-Lon-Schka, currently remain an important means of maintaining tribal solidarity.

1. Cultural and Historical Beginnings

The I'n-Lon-Schka dance and traditions came to the Osages from the Poncas and the Kaw, or Kansa, tribes in the mid-1880s after the Osage tribe had made its final move to Indian Territory from Kansas. At that time the Osages turned away from their old ceremonies and turned instead to the I'n-Lon-Schka. The tribe settled in three locations that are now Grayhorse, Pawhuska, and Hominy in Oklahoma. The band of Osages at Grayhorse (the Dwellers upon the Hilltop) received the I'n-Lon-Schka dance, traditions, and drum from the Poncas. The bands of Osages at Pawhuska (the Dwellers in the Thorny Thicket) and at Hominy (the Dwellers in the Upland Forest) received the I'n-Lon-Schka dance, traditions, and drums from the Kaws. These three communities remain the centers for tribal activities today and are the locations for the annual I'n-Lon-Schka dances.

As the Osages left Kansas for Indian Territory, they were a driven, confused, and divided people—divided by many moves and broken treaties and by interaction and intermarriage with the whites. Adding to their confusion after they moved into Indian Territory were pressures to allot their reservation and assimilate with other Indian tribes as well as whites. The following brief description of Osage history during these troubled times serves as a backdrop against which the I'n-Lon-Schka emerged as the Osages' most important ceremonial dance, celebrating the tribe's survival from the unrecorded past into the late twentieth century. It helped them through a time of great stress and spiritual confusion then, and it continues to serve as a cultural and spiritual reinforcement in the 1980s.

In 1803 the U.S. government through the Louisiana Purchase assumed jurisdiction and control over the country inhabited by

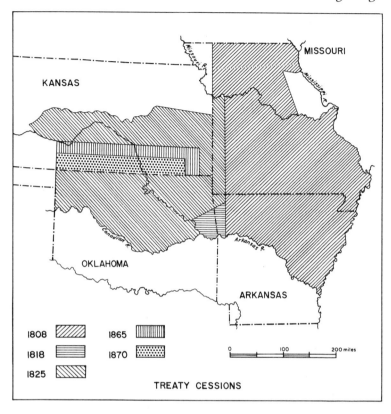

Map 1. Lands ceded by the Great and Little Osages
in treaties, 1808 through 1870. Adapted from
David Baird, *The Osage People,* p. 31.

the Osages. President Thomas Jefferson thought the new territory might serve as a new home for eastern Indians whose land was coveted by his nation's citizenry. Apparently little thought was given to the tribes, such as the Osages, who already occupied the vast Louisiana Territory and would violently protest these intrusions.[1]

The history of the Osage tribe following the Louisiana Purchase of 1803 was marked by a series of treaties with the United States in 1808, 1818, 1825, 1865, and 1870 (see Map 1) in which the Osage lands were progressively reduced and the tribe forced westward. The political importance and strength held by the tribe before those treaties eroded them were never regained. Although the Osages had been noted as great warriors in wars with the other tribes and against settlers and trappers, they fortunately avoided a major war with the United States, probably because constant war with both the eastern, immigrant tribes and the Plains tribes weakened the Osages' capacity to resist the advance of the white frontier.[2]

By 1872 the Osages had settled on rich lands in southeastern Kansas, but in that year the United States paid the tribe ten million dollars to move a final time to Oklahoma, then called Indian Territory. The new reserve was purchased from the Cherokees for seventy cents an acre with the proceeds of

Fig. 1. White Hair (Pah-Hu-Skah), head chief of the Great Osages, who signed the 1808 treaty and died shortly thereafter. Adapted by Chris Musgrave from a crayon drawing by Saint-Memin in 1804 upon White Hair's visit to Washington, D.C.

the Osages' Kansas lands, leaving some eight and one-half million dollars in the Osage tribal trust. The reservation extended from what is now Bartlesville to Ponca City and from the Kansas border to Tulsa; it later formed the largest county in Oklahoma, some 1,370,000 acres, but a small fraction of the tribe's once vast holdings. The Osages chose to move near the center of their new reserve and established their capital at Pawhuska, named after a later chief Pah-Hu-Skah, who had led them to this final reservation.[3]

In 1872 there was no way of anticipating two developments regarding the Osage land in Indian Territory. First, new cattle breeds with more tender meat came to dominate the

Fig. 2. A view of the Osage Agency at Pawhuska, Oklahoma.

Fig. 3. A view of the Osage wealth—stock and oil.
This scene is near Burbank, Oklahoma, where the large
oil fields were discovered. The bluestem grass that grows on this
rocky land makes good grazing for cattle and horses.

cattle industry. These breeds grazed better on Osage bluestem than on any other natural ground cover, making the western portion of the Osage reserve valuable as grazing range. Second, pocketed in the thick bed of limestone that underlay Osage land was something a lot more valuable than grass or cattle: enormous deposits of oil and natural gas. The discovery of the big oil pools under the Osage reserve led to dramatic changes in the tribe. The Osages changed from a people of hunters and warriors and a life of mobility to the settled life of landowners. It was the first time the government had been a part of a displacement in which the Indians would profit more from their new lands than they had from their old.[4]

Convinced of the need to create a new form of tribal government after coming to Indian Territory, the Osage tribe met in a grand council in January, 1881. A member of this grand council was James Bigheart, a full-blood chief of the Big Beaver band and an able and active Osage leader and politician from the 1880s until his death in 1906—a crucial period in tribal relocation and reorganization. He was one of several full-blood leaders who helped to steer the Osage tribe through the difficult

times of severalty. Understanding the vulnerability of the individual Osage to manipulation and swindle, he set about to prevent this by helping to organize the tribe into a unit. As the
Osage Nation, rather than as individual Osages, the tribe had a
better chance of getting results and hearings from the U.S.
government.[5]

Considered the prime mover in organizing the Osage grand
council and guiding its deliberations, Bigheart was rewarded for
his efforts in the tribe's behalf by being elected president of the
national council. In 1881 this same Osage grand council appointed a committee from within the council to draft a working
document for a new form of government and an Osage constitution. Two Osage political parties also emerged in 1881: the
Full-Bloods and the Mixed-Bloods. These parties still exist in
the 1980s.[6]

The Osage constitution that was finally presented to the
council was modeled after the Cherokee constitution, which in
turn had been modeled after that of the United States. It provided for the organization of the Osage Nation with a legis-
lative council known as the National Council; an executive
branch headed by a principal chief and an assistant chief, both
to be elected every two years by the popular vote of every
Osage male over twenty-one; a judicial branch composed of a
supreme court with justices to be elected—not appointed—for
two-year terms; and a sheriff elected from each district of the
tribe to help in providing criminal justice. The general tone of
this constitution proved that the Osages were trying to provide
a realistic, workable form of government for the tribe as well as
asserting themselves as a sovereign nation.[7]

Fifteen chiefs and prominent men signed their names to
the new constitution. Because of the support of this impressive
group of Osage leaders, tribal respect for the new government
grew. In the first election held in February, 1882, Governor Joe
was elected as principal chief and Strike Axe as the assistant
chief, and James Bigheart, Saucy Chief, Ne-kah-he-pon-ah, and
Claremore were among the fifteen chosen as legislators.[8]

The year 1882 was of special importance to the Osage in
quite a different way from the new tribal political organization.
As partial payment for their ceded Kansas lands, the Osages
were given cattle from the government. This was a small token

towards the government's promise to teach the Osages to farm. From three to five head of cattle were delivered to each family. At that time all of the land still belonged to the tribe, and an Osage could use all that he fenced. Although some Osages recognized the possibility of grazing and fattening the cattle on the bluestem grass and began ranching, most of the Osages opposed farming and ranching but supported the tribal leasing of these valuable grasslands to Texas and Kansas ranchers and farmers. Agent Laban Miles encouraged the Osages in this leasing of their natural pasturage, and the Bureau of Indian Affairs reluctantly agreed to this proposal after limiting the grange to the northern reaches of the Osage reserve. In December, 1882, the National Council agreed to the first grazing leases.[9]

In December, 1895, Osage Indian Agent H. B. Freeman, with the knowledge and support of the Bureau of Indian Affairs, approved a ten-year lease to Henry Foster of Independence, Kansas, for the "exclusive privilege of testing for and producing oil and natural gas on the Osage reservation." This proposal was presented to the Osage National Council in March, 1896, and by a narrow vote of seven to six was approved. Signed by James Bigheart and Saucy Chief, the lease was then forwarded to the Department of the Interior, where it received final approval, and drilling of the first oil well began.[10]

It was Bigheart's hope that finding oil and gas would prove to the tribe the advisability of holding their lands in common rather than giving in to the allotment of the reservation to each Osage individually, as the government had succeeded in doing with the other tribes in 1896. By 1906 he had proved conclusively that there were large oil deposits under the Osage reserve.

The Indian policy of the U.S. government in 1887 through the Dawes and Curtis acts of Congress was to allot to each Indian 160 acres of his tribal reservation. The surplus portions of these reservations were then opened to white settlement. The Full-Blood party, led by Bigheart and Black Dog, fought the allotment bills with all of their powers. They argued that the Osages were not ready for allotment of their lands, did not want it, and would not be able to agree on the division of land if allotment were forced on them. The Full-Blood leaders brought up old grievances as well, claiming that the Osages had not been paid enough for their Kansas lands and that names had been placed on the tribal roll illegally. In fact, their main issue was that there were non-Osages on the roll and those names would have to be deleted before allotment could be accepted.[11] Bigheart also noted that like the other tribes of Indians who had experienced government allotment, the Osages might very well lose their allotments after the reservation had been broken up.

Bigheart is credited with having held up the Osage allotment for over ten years, and as a result the Osages were exempted from the Dawes and Curtis acts. Understanding the Osage struggle to hold on to their lands, Agent Laban Miles wrote in 1890 that the Osages considered their reserve in Indian Territory as especially their own because they had bought it from the Cherokees and had paid for it and had been promised through treaty with the United States that it would remain their permanent home. He concluded that "the Osages deem themselves a Nation with a big N."[12]

However, by 1902 support for the Osage allotment had grown among both the Full-Bloods and the Mixed-Bloods. The entire tribe had profited by avoiding severalty as long as possible, but as Oklahoma statehood grew closer to reality, the time had come for Osage allotment—but an allotment with a difference. The final form of the Osage Allotment Act demonstrated the political wisdom of both the Osage Full-Blood faction and the Mixed-Bloods. In June of 1906 an allotment bill drafted by the tribe was approved by Congress. It differed from other Indian allotment acts primarily by reserving all mineral rights for the tribe as a whole (that is, the minerals under the top fifteen inches of soil) and by dividing the surplus lands among the members of the Osage tribe, thus preventing any wild settlement runs like that of the Cherokee Strip or the loss of any Osage land to white settlers. This separation of surface and mineral rights allowed the Osages to become the wealthiest tribe in the nation.[13] This great coup of the Osage leaders, in delaying allotment until they were able to save the land and its mineral rights for their people, allowed the Osages to maintain the I'n-Lon-Schka through their economic independence while other less fortunate Indian tribes had to give up their individual ceremonies.

From the very first, the proper enrollment of tribal members was a problem, but it became even more difficult as the wealth of the Osages increased, making citizenship in the Osage Nation a matter of great importance. A federal investigation of the Osage Indian rolls was begun in 1896 to remove those not entitled to Osage property rights. Records kept by the Catholic and Protestant churches during the nineteenth century became especially valuable in giving proof of parentage and Osage lineage. Proper enrollment, however, continued to be a problem through the final check of the Osage roll provided by the Osage Allotment Act in 1906. This roll was closed on July, 1906, with the provision that any child born to an enrolled Osage by July, 1907, could also be enrolled. After July, 1907, the allotment was permanent and those remaining on the Osage roll at this date were known as original allottees. No child born after that time would go upon the rolls or receive anything except by inheritance of the tribal wealth.[14]

The surface land was allotted individually, while the minerals were allotted collectively to the 2,229 legitimate Osages on the official rolls as of July 1, 1907. Each member received a tract of 160 acres designated as the homestead and restricted against sale for twenty-five years, and 498 acres of surplus land, for a total of 658 acres for each member of the tribe. Tribal funds were divided, and the pro rata share of each tribal member—$3,819—was credited to his or her account in the U.S. Treasury. The interest and royalties from the exploitation of minerals were distributed per capita to the members of the tribe quarterly, after agency operating expenses were set aside.[15]

In the Osage Allotment Act was a provision for the Osage reservation in the event of statehood. These lands became Osage County, with Pawhuska as the county seat, as Oklahoma gained statehood in November, 1907. Certain tracts were saved in Hominy, Grayhorse, and Pawhuska for communal property for those Osages wishing to continue the traditional village life. With these three 160-acre tracts the Osages provided for some continuation of the old traditional group living. The tracts continue to remain in the 1980s as places for any Osage to stay without cost for as long as he or she desires. These areas are referred to in each of the towns as "the Indian village."[16] And it is these "Indian villages" in Pawhuska, Hominy, and Grayhorse which serve as the settings for the annual I'n-Lon-Schkas.

The Osage Allotment Act established an Osage Council

composed of an elected principal chief, an assistant chief, and eight councilmen to be elected biennially. The council was also authorized to execute mineral leases, subject to the approval of the secretary of the interior. The former Osage National Council, which had been established in 1881 with three members from each of the five Osage districts, was abolished. The Osage Council established under the allotment act was amended in 1929 so that the officers of the council were elected quadrennially rather than biennially by an electorate composed of tribal members twenty-one years of age or over whose names appeared on the last quarterly annuity roll. In other words, only those tribal members with headrights or fractional headrights are allowed to vote in the tribal elections if they are over twenty-one. The Osage Council operates under neither a constitution nor a corporate charter. Instead, it functions like a board of directors of a corporation, exercising authority in leasing the tribal estate, in determining the bonus value of any tract offered for lease, in the use of tribal funds, and in the administration of the tribal reserves located at Grayhorse, Hominy, and Pawhuska.[17]

The bill also provided that the Osages could sell the surplus lands if they were able to satisfy the secretary of the interior that they were capable of managing their own affairs. Upon proof—usually simply the ability to read and write—of their capability to manage their own affairs, the Osages were issued their certificates of competency from the government. Also, each Osage, upon receiving his certificate of competency, could withdraw his trust fund, which had been kept by the government. Therefore, these documents became very important and were necessary before an Osage could control his or her property.[18]

Although the U.S. government had tried to protect the Osage Indians from unscrupulous whites, loopholes in the laws or ways around the laws were found by many whites who wished to take advantage of the Osage wealth. Some adult Osages were declared incompetent; young Osages often became wards of the local courts; wealthy Osages were murdered; wills turned up leaving Osage estates to local politicians instead of the Osages' families. Although the Osages were not allowed by law to sell their headrights, they could will them. However, if a non-Osage inherited such a headright, he could sell it. An active market developed for the Osage headrights in the 1920s for as much as $100,000 per headright.[19]

In 1917 the Board of Indian Commissioners sent George Vaux, Jr., to visit the Osage tribe. He described their problems as entirely different from those of other Indian tribes he had visited. "With the Osages the problem is the problem of riches," he declared. He was particularly disturbed that there had been no training offered to the full-bloods on the handling of large sums of money.[20]

The Osages were especially vulnerable, with some families receiving $65,000 per year in the bonanza. Many did not know what to do with their money, buying unnecessary items alien to their world, such as grand pianos, porcelain, silver flatware, and large houses. Merchandise was often sold at tremendous markups to them, and often Osages were tricked into enormous debts. It was at this time that the government decided that the Osages needed guardians unless they could prove their competency.[21] Everyone wanted to be a guardian, and guardianships became another way of bilking the Osage wealth. John Collier wrote: "In Oklahoma, individualized Indian estates were looted through a system of local white 'guardians' named by the Oklahoma courts pursuant to Congressional grants of power. To over two thousand Osages, with no experience in money economy and battened upon by the white population in the sixteen years following 1915, there was paid out in cash by the government, $265,000,000 in royalties from the Osage oil. . . . Ninety percent went 'downwind' of ruined Osages and corrupted and corrupting whites."[22]

The murder of wealthy Osages was also a part of the effort of unscrupulous whites to gain the Osage wealth. The "Osage Reign of Terror" is how Mathews and the newspapers of the time refer to that period in the 1920s when there were epidemics of Osage murders. This was the "most uncivilized, savage, period in Oklahoma history with the savages being the whites."[23]

Because of their economic wealth and security, many members of the Osage tribe have become integrated into society as they have received educations enabling them to enter professional fields. In the 1970s there were about three hundred full-bloods, one-half living in Osage County and the other one-half scattered. The predominant majority of the tribe in the 1970s and 1980s were the mixed-bloods.

At the crucial time of the Osages' removal to Indian Territory, they turned away from their old ceremonies, which were no longer serving them as well as they had in Kansas and Missouri. They turned instead to two new ceremonies which came from other tribes in the late nineteenth century: the dance the Osages named the I'n-Lon-Schka, and the peyote religion. These two ceremonies helped them in coping with their new life in both the white man's world and the Indian world and through a time of great stress and spiritual confusion.[24] Both the peyote religion and the I'n-Lon-Schka have served as cultural reinforcement through the twentieth century.

The peyote religion came to the Oklahoma Indians from the Mescalero Apaches in the 1870s and was formally incorporated as the Native American Church in Oklahoma in October, 1918. Although interest in this religion among the Osages was strong throughout most of the twentieth century, by the 1980s interest in the Native American Church declined among the Osages, with only some five fireplaces still in use.[25]

On the other hand, the I'n-Lon-Schka continues to flourish and remains as a great source of inspiration and strength to the tribe. Over three hundred dancers are present in the dance arenas of Grayhorse, Hominy, and Pawhuska on each of the three weekends the dances are held in June. Osages both old and young, full-blood and mixed-blood, join in the dance. It is the sense of the tribe's having survived and succeeded which guides the practice of this Osage ceremony. The I'n-Lon-Schka today becomes a celebration of the reflourishing of the tribe.

2. *The History of the I'n-Lon-Schka*

The Osages celebrate their dance named the I'n-Lon-Schka during the month of June. Agent Laban Miles reported in 1889 that for the Osages summer was the most important spiritual season. One hundred years later they continue to observe their form of worship as they continue to gather at Pawhuska, Hominy, and Grayhorse, Oklahoma. They celebrate in the grand tradition of a people who make any sacrifice demanded in order to keep their ceremonial. One senses that the spirit of the Lookouts and the Bacon Rinds and the Pawhuskas is still very much alive.[1]

I'n-Lon-Schka means "playground of the eldest son." The Osages place much importance on being the eldest—whether eldest son, eldest daughter, or eldest member of the family. The term *i'n-lon,* therefore, is used by the Osages for the oldest son in a family, while *schka* is the root for words having to do with sport or play.[2] It is a ceremony in honor of an eldest son in the tribe, who is chosen to be the Drumkeeper for a year, the drum being the sacred instrument in this ceremonial. The Drumkeeper may be as young as a boy or as old as a young man. For example, Pawhuska's first Drumkeeper, Ben Mashunkashay, was five years old in 1884 when he became Drumkeeper, and his grandson John Henry Mashunkashay became Drumkeeper for the Pawhuska I'n-Lon-Schka when he was twenty-one, serving in that office from 1972 to 1976. The acceptance of the drum by an Osage eldest son brings both honor and responsibility to him and to his family for the year he serves as the Drumkeeper. An elaborate dance organization is established after the new Drumkeeper is chosen, and there is a great deal of protocol, prestige, and tradition in this committee structure. (The dance organization will be discussed in detail in chapter 3.)

The I'n-Lon-Schka, however, is more than the recognition

of an outstanding youth of the tribe. It sets standards of conduct and ways of living for the tribal members; it is religious in context, revealing many of the religious beliefs and ideals of the tribe in the prayers, songs, and ceremonies; it allows the feeling of community to grow among tribal members; and it encapsulates much of the history of the tribe during the past century and thereby communicates, reinterprets, and reinforces tribal culture, customs, and beliefs to the tribal members.

Standards of conduct and ways of living that I'n-Lon-Schka participants are taught are respect for the drum, their elders, those in authority, those who have gone before them, and their fellow men, and the discipline to follow the I'n-Lon-Schka rules and traditions as dictated by I'n-Lon-Schka leaders and elders, such as abstaining from alcoholic beverages during the dances, dancing all of the dances, and not leaving the dance arena during a dance. Archie Mason, Jr., says that the I'n-Lon-Schka training prepares the participant both mentally and physically to take care of life's problems. Morris Lookout says that the proper administration and protocol of the I'n-Lon-Schka encourage conduct and courtesies that are becoming.[3]

Religious beliefs are expressed in the prayers before each dance and dinner throughout the I'n-Lon-Schka, addressed sometimes to Wah'Kon'Tah and sometimes to the Christian God. The reinforcement of tribal culture is seen in the dances themselves and in the traditional dress and is heard in the old and new family songs. Concern for the tribal future is demonstrated by the remarks of Chief John Tallchief during the 1987 Grayhorse I'n-Lon-Schka. He shared his concern for the proposed Prairie Parkway in Oklahoma and advised the Osages to vote against that legislation. He stated that the Osages need to preserve what they have and must continue to fight for sovereignty of their land.

The feeling of community which becomes a part of the I'n-Lon-Schka is shown in the concern and support expressed for persons and families who have experienced sickness, tragedy, and loss of jobs as well as in the sharing of the achievements and good news of tribal members. These families and individuals are mentioned in announcements and prayers throughout the four days of the I'n-Lon-Schka at both dances and dinners in each Osage village. For example, at the 1987 Pawhuska I'n-Lon-Schka, Town Crier Isaac Williams asked for all those assembled to pray for his nephew, who was sick. During a dinner at the same I'n-Lon-Schka, Browning Pipestem announced the accomplishments of his two sons. His eldest son, Wilson Kirk Pipestem, a champion runner, had placed in a National Olympic Trials meet. His youngest son, Francis Pipestem, Jr., was leaving to spend part of the summer preaching in Flagstaff, Arizona, and Colorado. In honor of his sons he gave a whole beef to the Jerry Shaw family for the 1988 Grayhorse I'n-Lon-Schka.

Because the I'n-Lon-Schka is the only Osage ceremonial with music and dance that has survived to the present, it is the dance that most tribal members will try to attend. It becomes a manifestation of tribal loyalty and continues to be a strong means of uniting the tribe and giving it a sense of identity. In recent decades it is still considered a serious, religious ceremonial dance by tribal leaders despite the loss of some of the text of many of the older songs and the loss of precise knowledge of the sequence of the songs and some of the rituals connected with the dance. As nothing is written and everything is maintained by oral tradition, songs and ceremonies that are not used are lost. In order to keep some of the old melodies from which the texts have been lost, often vocables are used today in place of the lost texts.

The drum is the center of the ceremony, both literally and symbolically, and respect for the sacredness of that instrument is one of the most important elements in the I'n-Lon-Schka. Four present-day Osage participants summarize their feelings on the significance of the drum. Morris Lookout says that the drum is the instrument that is used to communicate with the Great Spirit. It contains the thunder and the lightning and comes from nature. The Great Mystery—Wah'Kon-Tah—is also the Great Spirit, and the drumbeat is the calling to that Great Spirit. Archie Mason suggests that the drum is from nature and was made by the Great Spirit. The drum is the Osages' way of communicating with the Great Spirit and with each other at the same time. Archie Mason, Jr., says that the drum is the center and hub of the people, because the drum carries everything the people have—their songs, their life, their history. Ed Red Eagle believes that the drum carries the singers and the dancers and the tribe with it. They all follow the drum with the Drum-keeper, and they try to abide by the rules and rituals of it.[4]

In the nineteenth century American Indian tribes began to forget their individual tribal differences and to merge their cultures, producing a single pan-Indian culture that contrasts with Western European culture. The uniting of Indian cultures was further helped by the forced migrations of many tribes to special lands reserved for Indians by the whites, such as the Indian Territory, which later became Oklahoma. These tribes, forced to migrate and settle on lands reserved for Indians, often had had no previous contact with each other until they found themselves living side by side as neighbors. A cultural interchange and amalgamation resulted, with a dance of one tribe tending to spread to another tribe until all the tribes were doing a version of the same type of dance, such as the Prairie Indians' Grass Dance, discussed later in this chapter.[5] This cultural interchange and blending was experienced by the Osage tribe in the late nineteenth century as it settled on its final reservation in Indian Territory beside other Indian tribes.

In 1955 anthropologist James H. Howard used the term *pan-Indianism* to describe a supertribal culture that was especially prevalent in Oklahoma, where some tribes had lost their tribal distinctiveness and in its place had developed a nontribal Indian culture. Although the Osages lived in the center of this pan-Indianism, they participated in it to a much lesser extent than did poorer neighboring tribes (see Map 2 of the Indian Tribes of Oklahoma). The Osages shared their culture and received, in turn, new songs, games, and dances—the I'n-Lon-Schka ceremonial dance being one—from neighboring tribes (Fig. 4). They have been able to maintain this important dance through their economic independence, while other, less fortunate tribes have had to give up their individual ceremonies and become pan-Indian.[6]

Osage tribal members who are respected keepers of oral tradition concur in their separate accounts that the I'n-Lon-Schka came from the Poncas and Kaws, and they describe its coming to the Osage tribe in the following ways:

John Joseph Mathews, Osage author-historian, says that the I'n-Lon-Schka was originally a Dhegiha Siouan dance and

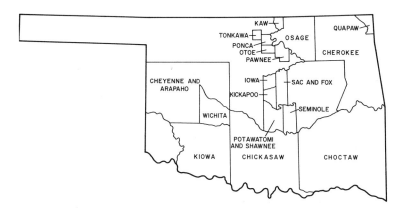

Map 2. Indian Tribes of Oklahoma. Reproduced from Arnold Marquis, *Guide to America's Indians* (Norman, Okla., 1974), p. 157.

Fig. 4. Early Osage I'n-Lon-Schka dancers.

came to the Osages through the Kaws and Poncas, co-members with the Osages of the Dhegiha division of the Siouan family.[7]

Marguerite Waller, Osage historian, says that because the Osages lived close to the Kaw Indian tribe when they moved to the Osage reserve in Indian Territory, Chief Blackdog II, son-in-law of the famous Chief Pah-Hu-Skah who helped in choosing this last Osage reserve, received a drum from the Kaw tribe for the I'n-Lon-Schka.[8]

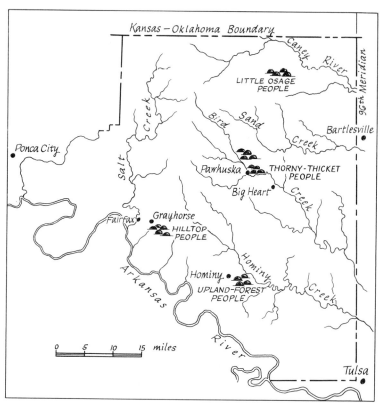

Map 3. Map of Osage County, Oklahoma. Adapted from John Joseph Mathews, *The Osages: Children of the Middle Waters,* p. 695. Note the location of the three villages where the annual I'n-Lon-Schkas are held—Pawhuska, Hominy and Grayhorse.

Ed Red Eagle, Pawhuska Dance Chairman for the I'n-Lon-Schka, says that the Osages have been dancing the I'n-Lon-Schka for over a hundred years. The drum was brought to them in Indian Territory, and they then dropped their Kansas ways. It took them several years to accept this new dance. In 1886 the Osages had to send a delegation back to Lawrence to accept and complete the buying and selling of their Kansas lands. It was just before that time in 1884 that the I'n-Lon-Schka came to the Hominy and Pawhuska bands from the Kaws. The Grayhorse band received the I'n-Lon-Schka shortly after the Hominy and Pawhuska bands had received it.[9]

Joseph C. Mason, in a letter to his son, wrote that John Blackbird, Sr., at age seven was the first Drumkeeper of the Osage tribe in the Grayhorse District and that the drum was presented by the Ponca tribe of Indians to the Grayhorse band. The exact date of this presentation is difficult to establish.[10]

Morris Lookout, Head Singer for the I'n-Lon-Schka during the 1970s and 1980s, said that when the Poncas and Kaws brought the I'n-Lon-Schka ceremony to the Osages in the 1880s—giving them the dance along with the songs—the Osages added their own songs and held the I'n-Lon-Schka for themselves as an Osage ceremonial dance. It is typical for the Prairie Indians to trade and buy each others' songs, and once traded or bought, those songs belong to the new owner and are not used by the former owners.[11]

During the nineteenth century the dance known as the Omaha Grass Dance became popular among the Northern Plains tribes. According to Clark Wissler, this dance was a modern form of an older Pawnee shamanistic ceremony called the I-Ru-Shka, in which the handling of fire and boiling liquids had a symbolic part. The term *i-ru-shka* has a double meaning. Literally, the idea is "the fire is in me," and symbolically, the meaning is, "I can extinguish the life in the fire" or can overcome the powers of other medicines. Also, the term *i-ru-shka* refers to a particular headdress worn by the dancers, called the hair roach (Fig. 5). The hair roach resembles the scalplock hairdo worn by the Osages before the late nineteenth century. Now a piece of deer tail is worn tied to the head to resemble the scalplock. In the center of the hair roach an eagle feather is attached; the feather represents men, and the red hair of the deer tail represents fire. There were elaborate ceremonies in the I-Ru-Shka in which certain men of the tribe were given the right to wear special articles of the traditional dress, such as the roach, bells, and feathers. Because information is fragmentary, it is only possible to speculate on the details of most of these earlier tribal dances and what features were distinct from tribe to tribe. However, the older form of this dance among the Osages did not include the fire handling of the Pawnees.[12]

Two important features of the Pawnee I-Ru-Shka cere-

Fig. 5. Archie Mason, former Grayhorse Dance Chairman,
wearing the traditional Osage headdress called the roach.

mony are the headdress of roached deer hair and the crow belt.
These came to the Omahas and presumably the Osages inci-
dentally as war honors, and the participation of their owners
would automatically bring them into the ceremony. Among the
Pawnees, however, these regalia distinctly belonged to the I-Ru-
Shka ceremony. According to Alice Fletcher, the Omaha ceremony is thought to be a derivative of the old Chiefs' Society,
entrance into which was graded by war honors. In the Chiefs'
Society a special song of praise was given to each distinguished
member. It appears that the Omaha dance consisted of honor
qualifications, individual songs, crow belts, and roached head-

dresses, all of which enter into the typical I-Ru-Shka ritual. The war associations are also a part of the Pawnee ceremony and probably came from the Omahas or Osages.[13]

The Omahas and Osages, in particular, contributed some special features to the Pawnee and Dakota ceremonies and in this new form gave them back to the Dakotas as a new organization. A retrospect of the I-Ru-Shka shows that some tribes received it three times in as many different forms. Therefore, this whole series of ceremonies, from the ancient ceremonies to the nineteenth-century Omaha Grass Dance, is little more than the successive work of four or five highly original minds. Archie Mason, Jr., says, "I know that this I'n-Lon-Schka came from other drums, other peoples, that we learned that dance from other tribes. . . . But as I look and research history, they [other tribes] too learned it. And all of a sudden it seems like it's a circle of knowledge . . . that it was already here but yet we learned it and yet it's still here and we're still learning."[14]

Although the Osage I'n-Lon-Schka is directly linked to the Ponca and the Kaw tribes, it also bears a resemblance to the earlier Omaha Grass Dance, a dance that the Poncas, Kaws, and other Prairie Indian tribes later received from the Omahas. As a tribe accepted a dance and made it a part of its culture, the dance changed in the transmission to become a distinctive dance of the recipient tribe.[15] Although the I'n-Lon-Schka still bears a resemblance to the Omaha-Ponca-Kaw Grass Dance, it also is distinctly Osage, blending Osage qualities, traditions, and culture with those of the tribes who had accepted the dance earlier. A complete description of the I'n-Lon-Schka follows in chapters 3 through 6, but I will briefly describe the similarities and differences between the Osage I'n-Lon-Schka and the Omaha Grass Dance here.

Clark Wissler states that the Omaha Grass Dance is a complex ceremony with an organization justifying its classification as a society. It has both a definite leadership, a variety of special officers with particular duties and distinctive regalia, and a considerable number of lay members. Although its function is chiefly social, and its meetings are distinctly social gatherings, it still has serious ceremonial elements. One of the main differences between the Osage I'n-Lon-Schka and the Omaha Grass Dance is the social aspect of the Grass Dance.[16]

The Omaha Grass Dance was associated with the He-Thu-Shka society of the Omahas, a society whose object was to "stimulate a heroic spirit among the people and to keep alive the memory of historic and valorous acts." The Omahas wore a long bunch of grass fastened to the belt at the back—hence the name Grass Dance. The grass represented the scalps taken by the wearer. As this dance was taken by the Yankton Sioux, the name He-Thu-Shka was retained as well as the bunch of grass at the waist, although the significance of the grass was lost. The Yankton Sioux carried a long bunch of grass as an emblem of abundance and the charity of their society of braves.[17]

The roach headdress remains a very important part of the traditional dress of those dancing in the Omaha He-Thu-Shka and the Osage I'n-Lon-Schka, and the ceremony of tying the roach to a boy's or man's head as he is introduced into the dance is an old tradition similar to those in the I-Ru-Shka, in which certain ceremonies gave a person the right to wear special articles of the traditional dress.

The Grass Dance is sometimes probably referred to as a war dance, even though it has never had anything to do with preparations for war, and in recalling historic and valorous acts of the past it by no means limited them to acts in battle. The Ponca Indians, one of the tribes from whom the Osages directly received the I'n-Lon-Schka, have a dance they call the He-Tho-Shka, also publicly referred to as a war dance. (Note the similarity in names between the Ponca He-Tho-Shka and the Omaha He-Thu-Shka.) This Ponca dance was originally performed by a society of Ponca men selected for their courage in battle and dedicated selflessness. It, too, was never associated in any way with a preparation for war or its aftermath (other ceremonials existed for those occasions), although the songs sometimes referred to the war deeds of the tribe's members. I have also heard the I'n-Lon-Schka referred to by some Osages and the white public as a war dance. This seems in the late twentieth century to be a popular term used generally for any ceremonial dance in which songs describe the feats of brave warriors, even though the ceremonials are not actually war dances by any tribal definition. Mathews strongly affirmed that though the I'n-Lon-Schka is sometimes referred to as a war dance, it has always been a peaceful social-religious dance.[18]

Both the Omaha Grass Dance and the Osage I'n-Lon-Schka were held in dance arbors—the arbor of the Omahas being round in shape while that of the Osages is rectangular today. The Osages first performed the I'n-Lon-Schka outside. Then a wooden structure called the Roundhouse (Fig. 6) was built in the early twentieth century fashioned after the early Quaker meeting houses in the East. It was entirely enclosed and had a limited capacity of about sixty dancers. As the number of dancers increased over the years, the I'n-Lon-Schka dancers were forced to perform outside again. In the 1940s the rectangular arbors were built—first of wood with brush roofs and then with permanent metal roofs and supports.[19]

Both the Omaha Grass Dance and the Osage I'n-Lon-Schka are opened with the "calling" of the dance by an appointed official with the title of Crier or Herald. The Crier calls the time for the participants to put on their traditional dress and also serves, in both ceremonies, to call out the tribal families and honored guests, deliver messages, and announce the events of the dance ceremonies.[20]

The drum in the Omaha Grass Dance is brought by the singers and placed at the side of the dance arbor, outside the circle of dancers, in an upright frame of four sticks. The singers are also seated outside the circle of dancers beside the drum.[21] In the Osage I'n-Lon-Schka, it is not the singers but an appointed participant, the Drum Warmer, who places the drum in the center of the dance arbor, and he is responsible for its preparation as well as its placement. The Osage singers are seated in a circle around the drum in the center of the dance arbor.

In both the I'n-Lon-Schka and the Omaha Grass Dance, the dances historically were performed primarily by warriors. They remain men's dances. Only since World War II have women been allowed to quietly dance in the dance arena on the edge of the men dancers' circle. In both the Osage and Omaha dances the men remain the more important dancers, dancing in free-style steps and body motions with most of the movements in the head and shoulders. Bone whistles are carried by three or four dancers in the Omaha Grass Dance, with one designated leader of the dancers signaling the Head Singer with his whistle if he desires the singing and dancing to continue.[22] In the Osage I'n-Lon-Schka, the dancer in an equivalent position of rank, the

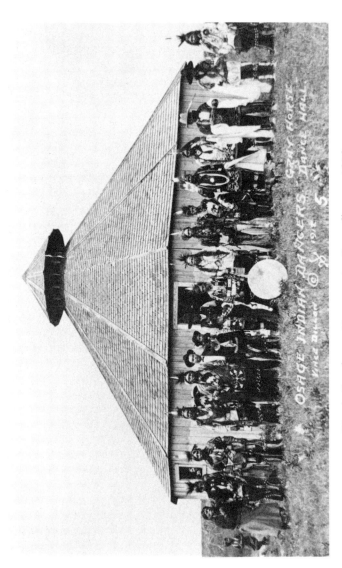

Fig. 6. Grayhorse Community Roundhouse, 1912.

head Tail Dancer, gives the signal for the continuation of the song and dance by raising his coup stick.

The position of Tail Dancer appears in both the Omaha Grass Dance and the Osage I'n-Lon-Schka. At the end of a song in the Omaha Grass Dance the singing and drumming stop briefly and then begin again almost immediately for a short chorus. It is at this point that one man, chosen for his ability as a warrior, "dances the tail," a solo encore. Only a man who has done some brave deed alone may be chosen as a tail dancer. He is honored by the other dancers by being so chosen. This feature of the Grass Dance had its origin in an honor dance, signifying that the dancer had conducted himself with courage and success in battle.[23] The position of Tail Dancer is still considered an honor among the Osages in the I'n-Lon-Schka, but the prestige now comes from being chosen as the best dancer rather than the best warrior. Presently in the I'n-Lon-Schka four to six Tail Dancers are chosen from each band of Osages by the respective Drumkeepers to dance the Tail Dance.

In both the I'n-Lon-Schka and the Omaha Grass Dance there are officials bearing ornamental whips for "driving the dancers"; they are the Whipmen. Any articles of costume lost in the Omaha Grass Dance must be redeemed with gifts to elderly men in the tribe and may be picked up by any of the dancers.[24] However, in the Osage I'n-Lon-Schka, only the Whipmen—the arena directors and liaison men for the Dance Chairman—are allowed to pick up lost articles on the dance floor, but they, too, must be given gifts before the articles may be redeemed. "Giveaways" are important aspects of both the Grass Dance and the I'n-Lon-Schka, with food, goods, horses, money, and other gifts given to people by the honored, as it is a part of Indian philosophy for an honored family or person at a ceremonial dance to give gifts to others rather than being the recipient.

Feasts were an important part of any Grass Dance and are most certainly an important part of the I'n-Lon-Schka. At the Grass Dance the man in charge of the dance decided who was to provide the feasts and then asked the Crier to notify them. The same people were never asked to provide for two successive feasts. Before the twentieth century, dog, considered a delicacy among the Prairie Indians, was often prepared at Grass

Dance feasts. When it was a part of the feast, a special dance by four selected men was performed around the dog bones.[25] To my knowledge, dog was not a traditional part of the Osage feasts. For the I'n-Lon-Schka, cooks are chosen by the Drumkeeper and his family. Cooks must prepare the food for the special feasts in traditional ways.

Although the importance of the drum and the important position of Drumkeeper in the Osage I'n-Lon-Schka are not found in the Grass Dance tradition, both the Osage and Omaha dances are similar in the positions of Crier and Tail Dancers, the practice of giving gifts or fines for dropped articles, the preparation of feasts, the style of dancing, the traditions of gift-giving and the honoring of persons in the tribe, the wearing of the roach headdress, and the seriousness of purpose of the dances. The I'n-Lon-Schka is similar to the Grass Dance in "stimulating a heroic spirit among the people and keeping alive the memory of historic and valorous acts." The similarity of names—He-Tho-Shka, He-Thu-Shka, and I'n-Lon-Schka—bear witness to the close relationship of these dances, and as a family, their characteristics set them apart from other ceremonial dances of these and other tribes.

The I'n-Lon-Schka is today a transitional form of the dance accompanied by the drum, bridging the gap between the old times now gone and the later times of change. The latter produced the closer reservation association of a number of neighboring tribes (see Map 2), with such cultural interchange as we have in this dance derived from the Grass Dance of the Omahas.

Also, the I'n-Lon-Schka today and in the past allowed for Osages of any blood quantum to take part and was not as restrictive as earlier dance societies, which were reserved for fullbloods. Therefore, the I'n-Lon-Schka takes in all Osages regardless of their blood quantum—an important aspect in the survival of this dance today with so many mixed-bloods and so few full-bloods.[26]

3. Traditions of the I'n-Lon-Schka

The I'n-Lon-Schka traditions have been handed down by word of mouth from one generation to the next. These traditions have changed very little during the ten decades the Osages have danced the I'n-Lon-Schka; however, there are a few changes in the old traditions, as well as differences between the three villages' adherence to these traditions. Pawhuska and Hominy allow more flexibility, while Grayhorse is more traditional in relation to the old rules. The intent of this chapter is to examine and compare the traditions as they now exist among the three Osage villages.

The traditional time for the I'n-Lon-Schka is during three weekends in June, which Mathews describes as the time of the "Buffalo-Pawing-Earth Moon, June, and may among the Dhegihan Siouan have had some ancient significance." The I'n-Lon-Schka is held at one of the three villages on each of the three weekends; usually the more traditional Grayhorse is first, followed by Pawhuska and then Hominy. Each village and band has its drum and Drumkeeper and a committeelike dance organization that plans and governs all three weekends of the I'n-Lon-Schka.[1]

The elaborate I'n-Lon-Schka dance organization is one of the most important aspects of the ongoing I'n-Lon-Schka each year. The organization is basically the same in each of the three villages. It is sometimes referred to as a society in newspaper accounts such as a 1975 article in the *Fairfax Chief* referring to the "Grayhorse Drum Society,"[2] but tribal members still refer to it as the "dance committee."

A Drumkeeper's first task after accepting his position is to appoint a Dance Chairman and the dance organization. The actual planning and organizing of the I'n-Lon-Schka is carried out by the Dance Chairman and his dance organization with the approval of the Drumkeeper and his family. Protocol, prestige, and tradition figure largely in the structure of this dance organization. The order and rank of those having an official part in the ceremonies are carefully respected by the other members of the Osage tribe. To be chosen or invited to serve in the elaborate organization of the I'n-Lon-Schka in whatever capacity—be it seventh cook, third dancer, Water Boy, or Tail Dancer—is an honor. Each man or woman asked to be a part of this dance organization has a designated place, position, and responsibility and follows the rules of that position under penalty of forfeiture or fine. John Henry Mashunkashay says that in thinking about the design of the I'n-Lon-Schka organization, with its different areas of responsibility, he believes it is almost perfect when all perform their duties.[3]

Dance Organization Positions and Responsibilities

The rules and regulations for the I'n-Lon-Schka were made in the 1880s by a council of Osages. The rules and regulations were discussed and agreed upon and then handed down orally from generation to generation. When a change was made or a regulation amended, the council held another meeting to make the necessary changes. There were no written rules or regulations. "These rules, as set out during the time of our forefathers, were very strict and everyone had to abide by them."[4]

The following were the original positions in the I'n-Lon-Schka dance organization as told to Joseph C. Mason by his mother and father, who were a part of the I'n-Lon-Schka in the 1880s when it became an Osage ceremonial dance:

> Drumkeeper
> Chairman of the Dance Committee
> Seven Dance Committeemen
> Two Advisors
> Two Tail Dancers
> Two Whipmen
> Two Waterboys
> Head Cook
> Three Assistant Cooks
> Smoker [The Smoker's position is an appointive position for life
>   and is not one of the positions selected by the Drumkeeper.][5]

In comparison, the 1974–75 I'n-Lon-Schka dance organization shows an increase both in number of positions and in the number of persons in the original positions.[6] But though it is larger, the dance organization remains quite similar to the original one described above.

Drumkeeper
Chairman of the Dance Committee
Eleven dance committeemen
Five advisors
Six Tail Dancers
Two Whipmen
Three Water Boys
Head Cook
Seven assistant cooks
Drum Warmer
Head Singer (drummer)
Nine men singers (drummers)
Six women singers
Town Crier (The Town Crier's position is an appointive position for life and is not one of the positions selected by the Drumkeeper.)

The present-day duties of each of these positions is well defined.

Drumkeeper (See Fig. 7)

The Drumkeeper, as noted earlier, is an eldest son, sometimes as young as six years of age. The Osages believe that the eldest child—whether male or female—is a blessing and that the eldest male child is even more special. The younger children in an Osage family accept the "specialness" of the eldest son. For example, John Henry Mashunkashay was the eldest son and the eldest grandchild and the only male child in his family. It was determined when he was very young that he would be Drumkeeper someday. As a child he was taught to respect, revere, and take care of the elders, and he remembers spending long hours listening and talking with them and being taught the old traditions. For example, his grandmother taught him the traditional methods of preparing foods from butchering to drying corn to selecting joncapins (water lily roots) for soup.

Fig. 7. The new 1975 Grayhorse Drumkeeper,
Curtis Oren Bear, with the palomino horse which he gave to
retiring Grayhorse Drumkeeper, King Bowman. The colorful
Indian blankets on the horse are a part of his gift. (The horse's
attendant is the Drumkeeper's brother, Jamison Bear.)

Mashunkashay was brought into the dance when he was eight years old, beginning as a Pawhuska dancer, then serving as Water Boy and working his way up in the I'n-Lon-Schka organization. After serving in Vietnam and recovering from wounds, he became Pawhuska's Drumkeeper at the age of twenty-one. Now he continues to participate in the I'n-Lon-Schka as an elder and coordinator of the singers. He is one of fifteen former Drumkeepers serving on Pawhuska's committee.[7]

The duties and responsibilities of the Drumkeeper and his family are numerous. With the acceptance of the drum comes the acceptance of a large financial obligation as well as a large commitment of time, which the Drumkeeper and his family must be prepared to assume. Although the Drumkeeper is officially responsible, his family advises him and shares in his responsibilities. Even families of modest means may accept the drum if they have the support of an extended family. It is a great honor to the Drumkeeper's family as well as to the boy that he is chosen to be the Drumkeeper.

First and foremost among the Drumkeeper's duties is to care for and protect the drum. The drum, about the size of a modern snare drum, when it is not in use is kept at the Drumkeeper's home. Because of the sacredness of the drum to the tribe and its importance to the I'n-Lon-Schka, the Drumkeeper is instructed to care for and to protect the drum at all times, to guard against its misuse during the I'n-Lon-Schka, and to see that it is not used during dances other than the I'n-Lon-Schka ceremonial dances. According to the advice of Joseph C. Mason, "The Drumkeeper should treat the drum as if one of the family, and any misuse of the drum will be noted by all concerned."[8]

Other duties of the Drumkeeper are to appoint all of the members of the dance organization—from the dancers to the cooks—after consulting with his family; to care for, lodge, and feed his I'n-Lon-Schka dance organization and guests during the four days of dancing in his own village; to furnish food supplies—called rations by the Osages—of staples, vegetables, fruits, and meats to the visiting I'n-Lon-Schka dance organizations from the other two Osage villages as well as to the singers and to visitors from other tribes and to notify his Dance Chairman when these rations will be given to the different groups;

and to ask his Dance Chairman to invite the Osages of his village to assist in the supplying of rations for the visiting groups.

The Drumkeeper must provide special meals during the year for the dance organization as well. These meals are given at the request of the Dance Chairman when it is time to begin the planning of the I'n-Lon-Schka dances and when it is necessary to communicate with the members of the dance organization on district or I'n-Lon-Schka problems and matters. Meetings are held following the dinners.

The Drumkeeper is responsible for seeing to sanitation, safety, availability of safe drinking water, and police protection during the four days of dancing in his village. Tribal police are hired for these ceremonial occasions to patrol the dance arbor grounds. Various pieces of traditional dress, valued at thousands of dollars, require some protection. The police also remove any disruptive or disquieting influence that would disturb the ceremonies.

The Drumkeeper at Grayhorse, in accordance with the old rules for the I'n-Lon-Schka, also must see that no raffles, collections, or lotteries of any kind are held during the dances, as the dances are ceremonial and not powwow dances.[9] However, at Hominy and Pawhuska such raffles and collections are allowed in order to help in the financing of the I'n-Lon-Schka in both villages.

Additional obligations of the Drumkeeper are to notify his Dance Chairman when he is ready to accept the drum after it has been passed to him; to furnish whips to the Whipmen; and to dance the entire four days during the I'n-Lon-Schka dances in all three villages. If the Drumkeeper is unable to take part, his father or his brother can take his place by wearing a blanket and sitting in his position.

Dance Chairman or Head Committeeman (Fig. 8)

Although the Drumkeeper and his family are officially responsible for and hold the position of honor in the I'n-Lon-Schka, it is actually the Dance Chairman who is in charge of the I'n-Lon-Schka ceremonies in his village and who is chairman of the dance organization throughout the year. Though he is responsible to the Drumkeeper and his family throughout his

Fig. 8. The Dance Chairmen of the Grayhorse,
Hominy, and Pawhuska I'n-Lon-Schkas in June, 1974.
L. to r.: Archie Mason of Grayhorse, Harry Red Eagle of Hominy,
and Ed Red Eagle of Pawhuska. All three men are cousins.

term of service, he is considered the most important individual in the I'n-Lon-Schka.

The Dance Chairman must plan and supervise the smooth performance of the I'n-Lon-Schka in his village. To do this, he gauges the length of each of the dances, signaling the Head Singer the number of songs or choruses needed.[10] He is also in charge of the individual I'n-Lon-Schka ceremonies such as the passing of the drum. As the master of ceremonies, he makes all of the announcements during the I'n-Lon-Schka, and he makes the final decision how to proceed when unexpected events interrupt the I'n-Lon-Schka.

The Dance Chairman is in charge of the dance organization meetings called during the year to make certain that the I'n-Lon-Schka in his village is well planned and well organized before June, to see that these plans are implemented, and to bring related I'n-Lon-Schka matters, such as requests or invitations from other villages or problems and news within his own village, before the dance organization. In the meeting the Dance Chairman listens to the opinions of the Drumkeeper and other organization members before expressing his own opinion, and a decision is usually reached by consensus.

Further responsibilities of the Dance Chairman include instructing the young people of his village on the meaning and seriousness of the I'n-Lon-Schka, explaining the importance of these dances to the Osage tribe through the years, and asking the young people of his village to show their respect for the drum during the I'n-Lon-Schka through their good behavior.

Dance Committeemen

The dance committeemen, selected by the Drumkeeper and his family, assist in all phases of the I'n-Lon-Schka and carry out the special duties assigned to them by the Dance Chairman. They are considered assistants to the Dance Chairman, and should the Dance Chairman not be present, the next man in rank on the dance committee takes over until his return. There is a very specific rank among the committeemen, from first to eleventh. Even in the seating at dances, they must sit according to their rank on the dance committee. These are honored men who know the dance and its traditions and are chosen to represent their village in the I'n-Lon-Schka ceremonies in all three villages.

Whipmen (Fig. 9)

The Whipmen, so called because of the braided leather whips they carry, serve as arena directors during the I'n-Lon-Schka dances. They are liaison men for the Dance Chairman and carry out his orders. One of their first responsibilities is to invite the dance organization members to the special dinners; to invite the other two Osage villages and other tribes to the I'n-Lon-Schka in their village when the dates have been set; and to serve as official messengers for the Dance Chairman.

As arena directors the Whipmen must watch for unruly or undignified behavior, both inside and outside the dance arbor, during the four days of dancing in their village and see that all dancers behave in a dignified fashion. For example, on three occasions the Whipmen responded to disruptive influences and behavior in the 1974 and 1976 I'n-Lon-Schka dances. At one of these dances in Hominy, a young woman deliberately tripped a little Osage boy dancing with his father. A Whipman immediately ushered the young woman to her bench, where she remained during the next several songs. This was all done very quietly and unobtrusively, and the dance proceeded undisturbed. On another occasion the Whipman from Grayhorse ordered a photography and recording group out of the camp for setting up floodlights and speakers inside the dance arbor before the opening dance. In the third case, at the 1976 Grayhorse I'n-Lon-Schka the Whipmen asked a photographer to stop taking pictures after the dances had begun.

The Whipmen must see that the Osage dancers and dancers from the visiting tribes all dance. In early times they actually used their whips on any reluctant dancers. Now they simply dance in front of a seated dancer until he moves out into the dance arena. In order to see that all of the participants are dancing during the dances, the Whipmen begin a dance by moving clockwise around the dance arena as the dancers move counterclockwise. In this way they can check the benches more easily.

By tradition the dancers are not allowed to pick up any dropped articles from the dance floor. The Whipmen are the

Fig. 9. Jerry Shaw, a 1975 Grayhorse Whipman
in traditional Osage dress. The braided leather whip in
his hand is a symbol of his position.

only ones allowed to gather up these articles. A fine is paid to the Whipman who retrieves a lost object before it may be returned. This Whipmen's post is probably a survival of a traditional duty to discipline those dancers who were careless or who were not well prepared for the dances.

Further duties of the Whipmen are to be in charge of the collection and distribution of food on the "give-away days," in which rations are dispersed to the visiting Osage bands, visiting tribes, and singers, and to be in charge of admitting and seating the various dance groups. As each dance group comes to an entrance of the dance arbor, it is met by the host village's Whipmen, who greet the group and then usher it to its designated place. Dancers arriving late must wait at an entrance until they are admitted and ushered to their places by the Whipmen.

Advisors

The advisors are senior members of the tribe who have been through all of the positions of the I'n-Lon-Schka dances and who know and understand all aspects of them. They are appointed by the Drumkeeper to give advice to him, to the Dance Chairman, and to the dance organization on matters pertaining to the dance regulations and traditions, on unexpected events that may occur during the I'n-Lon-Schka, and on problems and misunderstandings that might arise during the I'n-Lon-Schka or during the year. The advisors meet with the dance organization and the Drumkeeper at the special meetings called throughout the year.

During the 1974 I'n-Lon-Schka in Pawhuska, one of the Osage dancers suffered a heart attack and died on the dance floor at the close of the individual family songs on Sunday afternoon. The Dance Chairman immediately called his advisors together for their recommendation on the action he should take. As the dances were actually finished, except for the optional Cooks' dance, it was decided that "the drum should go into mourning" (be silent). The ceremonies ended then.

On the second day of the 1975 Grayhorse I'n-Lon-Schka dances, word was received of the suicide of a young Osage man well known in that village and the grandson of one of the Grayhorse cooks. The Dance Chairman consulted his advisors, paid his respects to the family of the young man, and made arrangements for the feast for the mourners. Only after this had been done were the dances continued. Many of the dancers did not enter the dance arbor until the Dance Chairman announced that he and his advisors had visited the family of the deceased and that arrangements had been made for the feast for the mourners. The I'n-Lon-Schka dances, once started, will continue except in the event of the death of the Drumkeeper or the Dance Chairman.

As the advisors are honored men of the tribe, they are sometimes asked to be in charge of certain ceremonies which are a part of the I'n-Lon-Schka, such as the introduction-to-the-dance ceremony, the giving of the opening and closing prayers of the I'n-Lon-Schka dances, and speaking in behalf of a family or person being honored.[11]

Tail Dancers

The Tail Dancers are appointed by the Drumkeeper to dance the encore or Tail Dances because they are among the best dancers as well as the outstanding young men in the tribe.[12] They must attend every dance at each of the three Osage villages and dance every dance. They are the only ones allowed on the dance floor during the Tail Dance after each song.

Traditionally, the host Head Tail Dancer is the only one permitted to raise his coup stick and signal for a repeated song and chorus. The Head Singer does not recognize any Tail Dancer who gives signals except the host Head Tail Dancer.[13]

Cooks

The Head Cook and her assistants are appointed by the Drumkeeper to prepare all the meals for the visiting Osage bands and the other visiting tribes. They prepare meals only when food is provided by the host Drumkeeper and his dance organization for the visitors. On a designated day during the I'n-Lon-Schka the cooks also prepare food for the host dance organization with rations provided by the host Drumkeeper. During the year they are responsible for cooking the meals for the special dinners held by the Drumkeeper for his dance organization. Often different members of the dance organization and leading families in the Osage tribe assist the Drumkeeper in supplying rations to the different groups during the I'n-Lon-

Schka as well as the various meals throughout the year. But the Drumkeeper is responsible for seeing that enough supplies are available.

Drum Warmer (Fig. 10)

The Drum Warmer is appointed by the Drumkeeper to prepare the drum, made of skin and wood, for the I'n-Lon-

Fig. 10. A drawing by Tom Russell of the I'n-Lon-Schka drum being brought into the dance arbor by the Drum Warmer and his assistant.

Schka dances and to see that it is properly placed in the center of the dance arbor for the dances. On the day of a dance, the Drum Warmer must heat or warm the drum over a fire all morning in order to tighten the drum head to the right tone.[14] In some cases the drum is placed in the sun to heat it, but heating it over a fire is the traditional way.

Water Boys

The Water Boys are appointed by the Drumkeeper to supply water to the singers and dancers. This "watering" is done by the Water Boys, who carry a bucket of water with a dipper around to each singer and dancer during the intermissions between the dance sets. The singers are "watered" first, and then the dancers. Each drinker after drinking pours a little of the water from the dipper on the ground according to the old religious belief that as you take away you must also give something back to Mother Earth.[15] The Water Boys start in opposite directions around the singers' circle and around the dancers' benches until they meet on the opposite side. The Whipmen check to see that the water buckets are kept full; the Town Crier is often designated to fill the buckets when the supply runs low.

Singers (Figs. 11 and 12)

The Head Singer—a good singer—is appointed by the Drumkeeper to be in charge of all of the singers and to be responsible for the music for the dances. His first duty is to establish the seating order around the drum, placing his singers with strong voices beside those with weaker voices and placing those who know the songs beside those who are learning them, thereby leaving nothing to chance.[16]

The Head Singer must lead the songs. This includes establishing the correct pitch of a song, setting the correct tempo of a song, indicating the times at which the Drummers will play the heavy drumbeats, and signaling to the women singers when they are to join in the singing. He must also establish the order and sequence of the songs in each set and be sensitive to the appropriate times for the inclusion of the classic songs in a dance.

As a part of his position, the Head Singer is responsive to the signals of a host Dance Chairman and host Tail Dancer for

Fig. 11. Osage Head Singer Morris Lookout
at the 1987 Grayhorse I'n-Lon-Schka.

repeats of a song or chorus. Today the Head Singer sits on the south opposite and facing the host Dance Chairman in order to see his signals. The old way was for the Head Singer to sit on the north with his back to the Dance Chairman. Morris Lookout reversed this position as the dances increased in size (Fig. 11). The Dance Chairman and Drumkeeper approved of this change as the "Dance Chairman needed his eye." [17] In most of the dances I have attended, the Head Singer has been opposite

Fig. 12. The singers' circle in the center of the
Grayhorse dance arbor. The men singers-drummers are on
the inner circle around the drum, while the women singers
are on the outer edge of the circle. Note the boxes of rations
placed around the singers' circle ready to be given away to
the visiting tribes in the afternoon dance.

and facing the Dance Chairman. But in the 1987 Grayhorse
I'n-Lon-Schka, the Head Singer sat with his back to the Dance
Chairman in the old manner.

Further duties of the Head Singer are to know, understand,
and be able to sing some 160 to 200 separate songs during the
four days of an I'n-Lon-Schka; to develop a tightly knit group of
performers who respect his leadership and each other and to
train his singers carefully in the songs, sometimes even holding classes before the dances for his singers; and to attend the
I'n Lon-Schka in all three villages.

The singers are chosen by the Drumkeeper. The men singers, serving as both singers and drummers, are the main performers, with the women singing occasionally on the choruses.
Often the Head Singer assigns songs to certain men singers
known for their strong, clear voices. These men, known as lead
singers, will then lead the songs they have been assigned. The

Head Singer or lead singer begins each song alone, singing a phrase in order to identify the song, the starting pitch, and the tempo for the other singers. After singing one short phrase, he is joined by other singers, who repeat the phrase that he has already sung before continuing the rest of the song. Because there are not titles to Osage songs (except in the case of the individual family songs, when the family name serves as a title), but only simple classifications such as war songs or prayer songs, it is necessary to hear a phrase of the song in order to know which one is to be sung. It is typical of many American Indian tribes to classify songs by types rather than by titles.

The Head Singer and the other singers are persons who are respected by the tribe, as they provide the music for both the ceremonial and the social life of the Osages. They are often publicly honored during the I'n-Lon-Schka with gifts of money, blankets, or food, or by being asked to have a part in a ceremony during the I'n-Lon-Schka. Head Singer Morris Lookout was asked to speak in behalf of Gertrude Sroufe, grandmother of the retiring Drumkeeper, King Bowman, at the acceptance-of-the-drum ceremony in Grayhorse in 1975. He expressed for Mrs. Sroufe and her family their gratitude for the many gifts bestowed upon them. In the 1976 Pawhuska I'n-Lon-Schka I heard Dance Chairman Ed Red Eagle publicly express his thanks to the singers in the following speech:

> While the Singers are still here before us tonight in the dance arena—the new and the old—I would like to thank them on behalf of the Drumkeeper, the committee and myself for their contributions of talent and the I'n-Lon-Schka. We have always understood and known that the drum is what gathers us, orients us, congregates us, and brings us here in this arena. Some of you young Singers who are here tonight have developed a talent which we appreciate. When you sing the I'n-Lon-Schka songs, it moves us, and helps to create the good spirit and feelings of the I'n-Lon-Schka.
>
> When you see us dancing in this arena, you see us in a congregation of three drums from the olden days of the Wah Sha'She [the Osage people]. I am addressing you now because you are needed and are valuable to us. Some of the men have been around the drum for many years, while others have been there only a short time. We appreciate your presence and contributions

which provide us with an opportunity to dance in the manner of our people. Jim Clark, Peewee Clark, Oliver Little Cook, Chick Kemble, Jim Kemble, Wilkie Eagle, Roscoe Conklin you are valuable to us now and in the future. [These men were singled out because they belong to tribes other than Osage, mostly Ponca.] Our hope is that you will continue the good work which your talent allows you to do, and which all cannot do. That talent is yours, and the blessing which comes from Wah'Kon-Tah I give to you at this time.[18]

This speech expressed the importance of these singers to the I'n-Lon-Schka and to the Osage tribe. Without the singers and their knowledge and interest in the old songs and music, the I'n-Lon-Schka could not continue. Their presence and performance are essential to the success and to the "creating of the good spirit" of the I'n-Lon-Schka. With the exception of Head Singer Morris Lookout, who is Osage, most of the singers around the I'n-Lon-Schka drum are Ponca Indians, as they have developed a fine reputation for singing the old ceremonial songs. Originally the Osages had all Osage singers in the early I'n-Lon-Schka, but throughout later years Osages have relied to a greater extent on the neighboring Ponca tribe as a source of fine singers. Traditionally these songs are passed down orally and are not written down. But in the 1970s and 1980s many of the singers made use of tape recorders to facilitate the learning and practice of the songs.

Town Crier

The Town Crier, an honorary position appointed for life, is considered important because of the encouragement given to the I'n-Lon-Schka by the Crier's calling. His duty is to call the dances and to "call out" honored individuals and families during the four-day ceremony. His calling is primarily in an Indian dialect, although he will call both the Indian and English names of a family or an individual upon request.

In 1976 the Town Crier was Isaac Williams, a Ponca Indian, who called in the Ponca language. Ed Red Eagle described Williams's installation and selection before the 1976 Grayhorse I'n-Lon-Schka, after the retirement from active participation of the former Town Crier, Raymond Tyndall, because of ill health. Williams was selected by those in the Grayhorse district who knew the responsibilities of a Town Crier. Once selected, he was invited to come to Grayhorse to call for the Drumkeeper and four Grayhorse families selected by the Drumkeeper— families who were active participants in the I'n-Lon-Schka. He came to Grayhorse during the week of the I'n-Lon-Schka and successfully called for the Drumkeeper. He was presented gifts by the Drumkeeper and his family before being given directions to the first Grayhorse family camp, that of Dance Chairman Browning Pipestem. At the first camp Williams called the Pipe-stem family names, received their gifts, and was then directed to the second, third, and fourth Grayhorse family camps, those of Cora Shaw, Gertrude Sroufe, and Ted Mashburn, Jr. At each camp the same procedure and courtesies were repeated before he was given directions to the next. After successfully calling for the four Grayhorse family camps, he returned to the Drum-keeper's camp and was confirmed as the new Town Crier. As he accepted this position for life, he sang a song of acceptance and gratitude. The other two Osage villages of Hominy and Pawhuska accepted and complied with his selection, and he was invited to both villages before their I'n-Lon-Schkas and was introduced to their Drumkeepers, Dance Chairmen, and dance organizations. Both villages helped him in learning the family names within their villages and presented him with gifts.[19]

Smoker

The Smoker, an honorary position appointed for life, is no longer used in the I'n-Lon-Schka. The Smokers in the earlier Osage I'n-Lon-Schkas played an important ceremonial role in-volving the lighting of the Drumkeeper's, Dance Chairman's, dancers', and singers' cigarettes, pipes, and cigars as well as the lighting of the cooks' fires for the preparation of the traditional feasts. The lighting of the fires was done with flint. At one time there was even a Smoker song in the I'n-Lon-Schka, and during that song the Smoker would light up. Perhaps the increased number of dancers was responsible for the discontinuation of this position and ceremonial role. Until the 1980s, there still re-mained a Grayhorse Smoker, Charles Kirk, who held the position although he no longer performed a ceremonial role and who apparently had no duties. The position was discontinued with his death in the early 1980s.

Traditions of the Drum

The tribal district as a whole owns the drum, as noted earlier. The Drumkeeper keeps it for the tribe and protects this sacred instrument from injury or abuse. Tail Dancers are instructed never to turn their backs on the drum. Dancers are instructed to show respect for the drum at all times. Younger dancers are quietly corrected by their elders if they should make the mistake of turning their back to the drum, or if they should become unruly on the dance floor.

In Pawhuska the tradition is for the dancers to wait until the drum has been properly placed in the center of the dance arbor before they enter. In Grayhorse the tradition is for the Grayhorse team to proceed with the drum and Drum Warmer into the dance arbor after all the visiting dance teams have been seated.

The drum must not be taken out of its village to which it belongs. An instance of the seriousness with which this rule is taken was described by Ed Red Eagle. In the 1970s the Osage Tribal Council and chief requested that the Pawhuska drum be brought to the Osage Agency for an Osage Nation powwow. The Pawhuska Drumkeeper with his Dance Chairman and dance organization refused the request. Red Eagle, who was Dance Chairman at the time, had a drum made especially for the Osage Nation and tribal council which could be used at the Osage Agency for powwows and tribal celebrations of a more social nature. But the Pawhuska drum remained in the village, and even the Osage Nation chief and tribal council respected the authority of the village over its drum.

Common expressions used by tribal members give evidence to the importance of the drum to the tribe: "The religion is in the drum." "The drum is in mourning." "I will put money on the drum" (money given to the Head Singer to be shared with the singers around the drum). "The song is on the drum" (a song accepted as a part of the I'n-Lon-Schka repertoire of songs).

Traditions Concerning the Four Days of the Dances

The I'n-Lon-Schka dances are held in large, rectangular, open-walled dance arbors. Originally the roof was made of brush, but the structure is more permanent today with steel beam supports for a permanent roof and sturdy bleachers on the east and west sides. The bleachers are for the spectators—members of the general public or the tribe who are not participating in the actual dancing (Fig. 13). On the ground level on all four sides framing the dance arena are benches, church pews, and folding chairs with the names of Osage families on the backs. These are the seats reserved for those families whose names appear on them.

Traditionally the I'n-Lon-Schka dances last for a period of four days during three weekends in June, beginning on a Thursday afternoon. The dances are held in the afternoons and evenings of each day except Sunday, when the dances occur only in the afternoon.[20] Rarely are the dances interrupted once they have begun. The only time the I'n-Lon-Schka is stopped completely, once it has begun, is at the death of the Drumkeeper or the Dance Chairman. The afternoon or evening dances of the I'n-Lon-Schka may be delayed for deaths of others in the tribe besides the Drumkeeper or the Dance Chairman, but the I'n-Lon-Schka, once started, will continue. However, if a death of a tribal member occurs in an Osage village before the I'n-Lon-Schka has begun, all plans and work for the I'n-Lon-Schka must stop until there has been a feast-for-the-mourners. The drum is said to be in mourning (silent) at this point, and it is released from mourning by the feast for the mourners and the cedar-burning ceremony.

Before the opening dance on Thursday, a Cedarman performs a cedar-burning ceremony. The Cedarman is appointed to this position for life by members of a certain clan who know the powers of cedar and the cedar-burning prayers. The evergreen cedar tree is a symbol of life to the Osages. This tribal position is not restricted to the I'n-Lon-Schka, as the Cedarman performs the cedar-burning rituals for those in mourning, for the sick, and for important tribal ceremonies and occasions. During funeral ceremonies the guests first wash and dry their hands and then parade past a container of smoking cedar. They

Fig. 13. A spectator, Emma Clark, at the 1976
Grayhorse I'n-Lon-Schka.

put their hands in the smoke and then touch their faces and
parts of their bodies. The smoke is said to purify the thoughts
and the body. It is also a form of prayer.[21]

The cedar-burning ceremony at the I'n-Lon-Schka involves
the Cedarman burning the wood chips in a metal pan as he
offers the prayers that have been entrusted to him for this ritual.
The host dance organization is "smoked" and blessed before
the Cedarman takes the burning chips around the dance arbor,
purifying the dance floor with his prayers and the smoke of the
burning wood. This "smoking" brings blessings upon those
who dance upon this floor and imparts a good spirit to the
I'n-Lon-Schka.

In Grayhorse, Archie Mason is the Cedarman for life. This
position was given to him by Helen Pratt Matin, a member of
the same clan as Mason. She taught him the special prayers and
proper procedures for this ceremony, such as how to select,
light, and carry the cedar. Mason is able to perform the cedar-

burning ceremonies for the Osages in the other districts if he is invited to do so. In Pawhuska there is no specially designated Cedarman for life as in Grayhorse, and this position is given to a Whipman instead.

The I'n-Lon-Schka is opened on Thursday afternoon by a prayer and welcome from the Dance Chairman.[22] The actual dancing then begins. This same opening welcome is repeated Thursday evening for the new people in attendance. On Friday and Saturday the dances continue with an increased number of dancers at each dance, culminating in the largest gathering at the Saturday evening dance. Usually rations are given on Friday evening to the two Drumkeepers of the visiting Osage bands. On Saturday afternoon rations are given to the singers and the visiting tribes other than Osages. On both occasions these rations are given during the breaks between the different dance sets (Fig. 11).

It is customary on Saturday afternoon or evening for each visiting Drumkeeper to express his appreciation for the hospitality and courtesies extended to him and to his dance organization by the host village Drumkeeper and dance organization. Typical of such a speech is the following one by Ed Red Eagle on behalf of his Drumkeeper: "I bring thanks on behalf of my Drumkeeper for the meal this noon, the food and the rations. We have prayed over it, broken bread and have found your hospitality and kindness very encouraging. Thank you."[23]

Gifts sent on Friday and Saturday by absent members of the host band are announced by the Dance Chairman. For example, in the 1975 Saturday afternoon dance in Grayhorse, the Dance Chairman announced that Darnell Kidd was unable to be there and had sent a gift of money to be "placed on the drum" (to be divided among the musicians).

Persons may be honored by the tribe at any spot in the I'n-Lon-Schka dances. In the 1976 Grayhorse I'n-Lon-Schka a Crow Indian woman from Montana, Mrs. Not Afraid, was honored during the Saturday afternoon dances. She had brought food to the Cora Shaw family camp because of a death in that family the previous week. The Shaw family asked that two songs be performed in her honor to show their appreciation. Her chair was placed in the center of the dance arena as these dances were performed in her honor. During the Saturday evening dance of that same day a Catholic nun, Sister Ursula, from Skiatook, Oklahoma, was honored for her fifty years of service in the Oklahoma schools. Dance Chairman Browning Pipestem, assisted by a Catholic priest, Father Gavin, made the presentation.[24]

On Sunday afternoon the individual family songs are sung. These songs honor and recount the deeds of the great leaders within the Osage families. Each family or individual whose song is being sung dances during that song, joined by friends of the family. Following each family song, it is customary for the family being honored by the song to give gifts. The gifts are given to honor the song and the family. Mathews thinks that this dance might once have been called the Smoke Dance, as the pipe was smoked by both the giver and the receiver of the gifts.[25]

The gifts are given to friends; institutions such as hospitals, schools, and churches; organizations such as the Grayhorse Ladies Organization, the Grayhorse War Mothers, and the Grayhorse Community Organization; officials in the I'n-Lon-Schka such as the Drumkeeper, Head Singer, Dance Chairman, Whipmen; and persons whom they feel deserve special recognition. As the family members honored by a family song leave the dance circle after a dance, many go directly to individual dancers seated on the dance benches, as well as to individuals in the audience, and give them gifts of money.[26] This is all done very quickly and quietly by both the men and women of the family honored by a family song. The public presentations of gifts from a family following their family song are announced by the Dance Chairman, and the persons receiving these gifts are called forward to accept them.

The gifts vary from money to blankets, quilts, groceries, and provisions for next year's I'n-Lon-Schka. In the 1880s horses were common gifts at these "give-away days."[27] Typical gifts given at the 1976 Grayhorse I'n-Lon-Schka, announced by Dance Chairman Pipestem, were a hog to the Grayhorse Drumkeeper for the 1977 I'n-Lon-Schka from Mr. Blackbird, grandfather of Girard Fish, who was unable to be present; a beef to the Pawhuska and Grayhorse Drumkeepers for the 1977 I'n-Lon-Schkas from Cody Tucker; and money to each of the three Drumkeepers from the mother of Johnny Williams, who was unable

to be there as he was serving as a medic in Winnebago, Nebraska, where there were few doctors and little medical service
available. Often verbal thanks are expressed by a representative
of the family to everyone who has joined in his family dance.[28]

On each of the four days of the I'n-Lon-Schka dances,
warning or signal bells are rung by the Town Crier to call the
dancers to the arbor. The first bell rings some forty-five minutes
before the dance is to begin. This is the first call to participants
and the signal to begin dressing for the dance. The men who
participate in the I'n-Lon-Schka dances must wear the traditional Osage dress before being admitted to the dance floor.[29]
Women, however, may dance in the traditional dress or with
only a blanket or shawl over contemporary street dress. The
traditional dress for both men and women will be described in
detail in chapter 6.

Bells ring at intervals until the final bell, which continues
its tolling, calling the participants to the dance arbor. At this
point the processions of dancers from the three districts and the
visiting tribes form and begin to proceed to the dance arbor.
The entrance of the dancers into the arbor varies in the three
villages.[30] At Hominy and Pawhuska the first procession to
reach the dance arbor is that of the host Drumkeeper, his Dance
Chairman, the dance committeemen, Tail Dancers, and Water
Boys. Before any of the groups are admitted into the dance arbor, the Drum Warmer brings in the village drum and places it
correctly in the center of the dance arbor. After the drum is in
place, the singers-drummers enter and take their places in the
circle around the drum. The women singers next seat themselves behind the singers-drummers (Fig. 11). At Grayhorse
the visiting groups are admitted into the dance arbor before the
Grayhorse group enters with the drum and Drum Warmer. The
singers at Grayhorse are also seated before the drum is brought
in, and the singers' circle opens to allow the drum to be put into
position.

The host Whipmen greet the dance processions and individual dancers at the entrances of the dance arbor and usher
them to their designated places. The Dance Chairman is seated
first, followed by the Drumkeeper and his dancers in order of
their position in the dance organization. The Whipmen seat

themselves at either end of their district's dance group. Each man puts at his place on the bench a folded blanket which serves both as a cushion and as a seat reservation.

Traditionally the host Dance Chairman and his group sit in the center of the north side of the dance arbor. The visiting tribes other than Osages are seated on the south. The two other Osage districts are seated on the east and west. The host Whip-men must arrange for the benches and see that there are enough seats for the dancers at each dance. These benches are placed in single rows around the dance arena. If there are too many dancers from the visiting tribes to be seated in the single row of benches, then double rows are placed on the south. Never are there double rows of benches placed for the three Osage groups; theirs must remain in a single row. Women are seated in the dance arena if there is room; otherwise, they must sit outside the dance arena (Fig. 14).[31]

Camps are set up around the grounds of the dance arbor during the four days of the I'n-Lon-Schka. Each visiting Osage

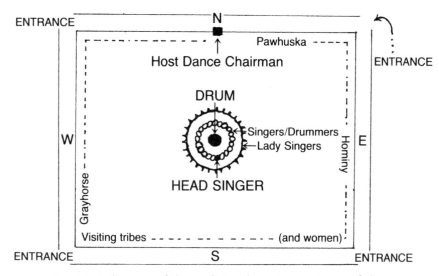

Fig. 14. A diagram of the traditional seating positions of the various groups of Dancers at the Osage I'n-Lon-Schkas. The host Dance Chairman and dancers are seated on the north side.

district, the host Drumkeeper, the host Dance Chairman, the host advisors, various Osage families of the host district, and the visiting tribes all have camps. It is customary for meals to be given in the host camps to which visitors, guests, and dancers from the different groups are invited. The host Drumkeeper is responsible for furnishing a large share of the food for these meals. However, the Osage families of a village hosting the I'n-Lon-Schka feel that the drum is not just the Drumkeeper's, but theirs also, and accordingly they make contributions of food, money, and work during the I'n-Lon-Schka in their village.

After the rations are supplied to the visiting Osage bands, visiting tribes, and singers, the host cooks prepare the food for them. Those selected as cooks are traditionally the only ones allowed to prepare the food, and that task is both an honor and a responsibility. The cooks prepare many of the traditional Indian foods such as fried bread, corn soup, beef soup, ground corn, meat gravy, grape dumplings, and fried meat pies in a manner handed down by their mothers and grandmothers. The meat for the barbecues is also prepared in the traditional way, with a large piece of meat being partially sliced through in small diagonal slices. Kettles of hot, boiling fat for the fried bread and meat pies are always a part of the camp scene. In earlier times the Smoker of a village would light the cooks' fires during the I'n-Lon-Schka in his village. This tradition is no longer followed, and the cooks light their own fires. Heavy-laden tables with Indian foods and typical American potluck dishes are found at each camp. Soft drinks are served, as alcoholic beverages are inappropriate, and indeed are not allowed at any of the I'n-Lon-Schka activities.

These "sit-down" dinners—opened with prayers, introductions of the various I'n-Lon-Schka officials, and short speeches of welcome—offer an opportunity for visiting, socializing, and fellowship. Enmities are pushed aside during the days of the I'n-Lon-Schka, with friends and visitors welcomed to a general kind of "open house" in all of the camps. The support, community, and good spirit witnessed in the four days of the I'n-Lon-Schka in each village are achieved through the combined hospitality offered at the meals; the honoring of visitors and tribal members; the graciousness shown in the expressions of thanks from the visiting Drumkeepers, dance organizations, and visitors; the many kindnesses such as the expressions of sympathy for those who have lost members of their families; and the respect for the many traditions of the I'n-Lon-Schka.

Special Dinners and Meetings

Special dinners are given by the Drumkeeper and his family during the year for the Dance Chairman and the entire dance organization. These dinners are similar to those held during the I'n-Lon-Schka in that they include both traditional Indian food and standard American fare prepared by the cooks, are "sit-down" dinners, and are opened with prayers and introductions. They differ in that they are open only to members of the dance organization. These special dinners are followed by meetings. Traditionally no women members of the dance organization have been allowed to attend or to have a voice in the meetings, but they have been allowed to attend the dinners. This is true today only in Grayhorse, since Pawhuska and Hominy now allow the women members of the dance organization to attend both the dinners and the meetings and to have a voice in the meetings.

Because one of the first acts of a new Drumkeeper is to select a Dance Chairman and the other members of the dance organization, the first special dinner is planned after the Drumkeeper and his family have decided upon the persons to fill the various positions in the dance organization—often in consultation with the new Dance Chairman. At the dinner a list of the new dance organization positions is read, and the persons named to these positions are asked to accept. Since it is a great honor to be asked to serve in the dance organization, the acceptance is almost automatic from those invited to serve. Usually those invited are a group of men and women who have been a part of the I'n-Lon-Schka dance organization in the past and understand the responsibilities of the positions. They also understand that they represent their district in the I'n-Lon-Schka ceremonies. Each person accepting a position from the new Drumkeeper is "paid" by him, receiving gifts usually of blankets, shawls, or food. This particular dinner is often held during the actual days of the I'n-Lon-Schka.

Another dinner-meeting planned by the Drumkeeper for

the Dance Chairman and his dance organization is for the purpose of deciding on the next I'n-Lon-Schka dates in their village.
This dinner-meeting is at no set time but is usually held in the
late fall or winter. (Often these I'n-Lon-Schka dates have been
discussed by the three Dance Chairmen before these dinner-
meetings in the three villages.) The Grayhorse district usually
holds this particular dinner-meeting first. After the dates for the
I'n-Lon-Schka have been discussed and chosen in the meeting,
the Grayhorse Whipmen are sent to the Pawhuska and Hominy
Drumkeepers to invite them and their dance organizations to
the Grayhorse I'n-Lon-Schka. Also at this time formal invitations to the Grayhorse I'n-Lon-Schka are extended by the Grayhorse Whipmen to the Ponca, Otoe, Kaw, and Pawnee tribes.
After receiving and accepting the invitation from the Grayhorse
Drumkeeper and dance organization, the Pawhuska and Hominy Drumkeepers and dance organizations hold their respective
dinner-meetings to select their I'n-Lon-Schka dates. As their
I'n-Lon-Schka dates are set, the same procedures, as described
in the Grayhorse example, are followed in each of the other two
Osage districts.

During the year other special dinner-meetings are given by
the Drumkeeper for his dance organization in order to complete
plans for the I'n-Lon-Schka in that district; to relay information
on I'n-Lon-Schkas in the other districts; and to solve problems
that arise within their district in relation to the I'n-Lon-Schka.
These dinner-meetings help in drawing a district together, keeping its members informed, and giving them a sense of tribal
identity.

Another special dinner given by the Drumkeeper, Dance
Chairman, and advisors is the feast for the mourners, as described on page 44. This feast is given at the death of a tribal
member in an Osage district or a relative of a member of the
I'n-Lon-Schka dance organization in a district. There cannot be
any planning or activity related to the I'n-Lon-Schka until the
mourning family has been taken care of through this feast. The
drum "goes into mourning"—is kept silent. The Drumkeeper
arranges for the feast for the mourners assisted by his Dance
Chairman, who helps to collect the food.

Before the feast for the mourners the cedarman conducts a
cedar-burning ceremony in which all the dance organization

members are smoked before the cedar smoke is carried around the arbor. The fire of cedar is prepared in a small pan and lighted only with flint in the old traditional way. This cedar-burning ceremony generally is conducted at dawn on the day of the feast for the mourners. According to old tribal beliefs, the purifying smoke of the cedar, combined with the special prayers, protects the tribal and family members from the spirits and allows the spirit of the deceased to go peacefully into the spirit world. After following this procedure for the ending of a mourning period, the drum is released from mourning (and silence), plans may once again continue for the I'n-Lon-Schka, and the family of the deceased is expected to "put aside" its grief and rejoin the tribe members in tribal activities.

I'n-Lon-Schka Ceremonies

Passing of the Drum

The beauty, dignity, and religious spirit of the I'n-Lon-Schka are enhanced by the ceremonies which are an inherent part of it, and the careful observance of the traditions which are associated with these ceremonies. The ceremonies described here are the passing of the drum, the acceptance of the drum, and the introduction to the drum.

The passing-of-the-drum and the acceptance-of-the-drum ceremonies are performed after a new Drumkeeper has been chosen.[32] The drum is often kept for a period of several years, but at the end of each year a decision is made by the Drumkeeper to keep the drum for another year or to pass the drum to a new Drumkeeper. In Grayhorse, if the decision is made to pass the drum, the Drumkeeper talks over the possible new Drumkeepers and their families with his family and friends. Three prospective new Drumkeepers are chosen. On the last day of the I'n-Lon-Schka the Dance Chairman, Town Crier, and Whipmen go to the first of the three prospective Drumkeepers to ask him and his family to accept the Drumkeeper's position. If he accepts, he will be the new Drumkeeper, and the other two prospective Drumkeepers are not approached.

In Pawhuska, if the decision is made to pass the drum, the Drumkeeper, Dance Chairman, and dance committeemen and advisors hold a breakfast meeting on the morning of the last day of the I'n-Lon-Schka ceremonies. The Drumkeeper informs his dance committee that he will no longer be the Drumkeeper and that he has selected a new eldest son and his family for this position and honor. If the candidate selected by the Drum- keeper accepts, he will be the new Drumkeeper. He shows his acceptance by giving gifts to the three representatives of the old Drumkeeper, who are the two Whipmen and the Town Crier. When the Town Crier cries the news of the acceptance and all three return with their gifts—usually blankets—the rest of the village knows that the drum has been accepted.[33] If the Drum- keeper's choice refuses, it becomes the turn of the Dance Chair- man to make the next choice of a candidate and his family for this position. The first Dance Committeeman or Head Tail Dancer would have the next choice if the Dance Chairman's choice refuses. The Whipmen and Town crier carry the invita- tion to the new prospective Drumkeeper.

In all three villages the Drumkeeper is chosen because of his work and position in the tribe, as well as for his family heri- tage and family's position in the tribe. Many families are glad to see their young men honored in this way, believing that the position of Drumkeeper instills a sense of responsibility and maturity that helps a boy along the path toward manhood. With the acceptance of the position by a new Drumkeeper, a short ceremony is held for the passing of the drum following the fam- ily and individual songs. This short ceremony is little more than an announcement by the Dance Chairman that the drum has been passed to a new Drumkeeper. After the announcement the drum is taken by the Town Crier, Drum Warmer, and Whip- men to the new Drumkeeper. The acceptance-of-the-drum ceremony the following June is the more important of the two ceremonies and is actually the completion of the passing-of-the- drum ceremony.

Acceptance of the Drum

Although the acceptance of the drum most commonly takes place on the first afternoon of the I'n-Lon-Schka, it can be done at any time during the four days according to the wishes of the new Drumkeeper and his family. For example, this cere-

mony was held on Friday afternoon in 1975 because of delays
in the completion of handwork on the gifts, and the absence of
some of the dancers. The ceremony incorporates the honoring
of tribal members, the expression of thanks to those who have
served in the past, the giving of gifts by those being honored,
the formality and dignity of the speeches of thanks and acceptance, and the participation and support of all generations
for the tribe.

The acceptance of the drum at Grayhorse on June 6, 1975,
was typical or traditional for such a ceremony. At 2:30 in the
afternoon the bell tolled the final call for the dancers, and the
traditional dance procession, with two exceptions, formed in
the camp of the new Drumkeeper, Curtis Oren Bear of the
Jamison Bear family. The two exceptions in the procession were
at the front and at the end. At the front was a man leading
a beautiful palomino quarterhorse, blanketed with a brightly
striped Indian blanket and a blanket trimmed with Osage ribbon work (Fig. 7). At the end of the procession were eight young
Osage women dressed in the traditional Osage wedding dress.
These women were called "brides" because they were wearing
the Osage bridal dress and not because they were actually to be
married. All were related to the new Drumkeeper. (A full description of the traditional Osage wedding dress will be given in
chapter 6.) Upon reaching the dance arbor, all members of the
procession, with the exception of the horse and its attendant,
were ushered to their places within the arbor. The horse remained outside the arbor because the dance floor had been
blessed. The other dance processions were then ushered in and
seated, and the acceptance-of-the-drum ceremony began.

The new Drumkeeper and his family joined the new Dance
Chairman in the center of the north side of the dance arbor. The
Dance Chairman announced that Curtis Oren Bear accepted
the drum and that he and his family would give gifts to the former Drumkeeper, King Bowman, and his I'n-Lon-Schka dance
organization in token of this acceptance. (The giving of these
gifts constitutes the acceptance of the drum by the new Drumkeeper.) Each recipient of a gift was called forward by the
Dance Chairman to receive his gift and to be thanked for his
service on the former I'n-Lon-Schka dance organization.

The first to be honored with a gift was former Drumkeeper King Bowman. The beautiful palomino was presented to him at the entrance to the dance arbor. Next to be recognized and to receive gifts were the members of Bowman's entire I'n-Lon-Schka dance organization, from the dance committeemen to the Water Boys, who were called forward individually. The gifts presented to them were most commonly in the form of blankets, shawls, and rations, but seldom money.[34]

Perhaps the most unusual gifts, aside from the palomino, were the colorful traditional Osage wedding dresses worn by the Osage girls who had been a part of the Grayhorse dance procession. These dresses were given to special women who had been important in roles in the former I'n-Lon-Schka dance organization. Some of the women so honored were Gertrude Sroufe, grandmother of King Bowman; Barbara Bowman, mother of King Bowman; and Lorena Mashburn, Head Cook in both the former and new I'n-Lon-Schka dance organizations. As each woman honored by a gift of a traditional wedding dress was called forward, a girl in this dress stepped forward to meet her. After greeting the Jamison Bears and the new Dance Chairman, Browning Pipestem, the recipient of the Osage wedding dress then led the girl to the edge of the dance arbor, where she removed the dress from the girl (who wore it over everyday clothes), carefully folded up each piece of the dress, and then resumed her seat. The traditional Osage wedding dress, decorated with a large amount of Osage ribbon work, beadwork, and finger weaving by the women of the tribe, is a source of great pride to the owner.

Formal speeches were next given by different men in the tribe. The new Drumkeeper was introduced by an advisor who gave a résumé of the reasons for his selection. Ed Red Eagle made a speech in behalf of Rose Pipestem, mother of the new Dance Chairman, expressing her gratitude and humility of the honor given to her son in his new position as Dance Chairman. Head Singer Morris Lookout made a speech in behalf of Gertrude Sroufe, expressing thanks and appreciation for the gifts she and her family had received as well as expressing how humbled and honored they were to receive so much. At Grayhorse and Pawhuska, women without husbands or older men in their families rarely speak for themselves. Instead, they ask a leader or an elder of the tribe to speak for them in the I'n-Lon-Schka ceremonies. As the man makes the speech in her behalf, the woman stands quietly beside him.

After the gifts were given, speeches made, and the drum officially accepted by the new Drumkeeper, the passing-of-the-drum and the acceptance-of-the-drum ceremonies were completed. The drum had passed to a new guardian. The new Drumkeeper's first official duty was to open the first I'n-Lon-Schka dance of the afternoon. He did this by going to the singers-drummers' circle, receiving a drumstick from the Head Singer, and striking the first drumbeat of the afternoon dances. The drumstick was returned to the Head Singer, and the 1975 Grayhorse I'n-Lon-Schka dances were officially underway. Because of the length of the ceremonies and speeches, the actual dancing during this dance was very brief.

Introduction to the Dance

Another important tradition of the I'n-Lon-Schka is the introduction-to-the-dance ceremony, which allows a boy or a man to become a part of the dance. There is no certain age specified for this ceremony, with ages ranging from boys as young as toddlers to adult men (Figs. 15 and 16). Before a boy can be a part of the dance, he must understand what clan he is from and his Indian name. Not all Osages in the 1980s have an Indian name, and only those who desire one have the name-giving ceremony. But to be introduced to the dance a boy must have an Indian name, given by someone within the clan who is designated for such a role. Before the ceremony the significance of the roach—the traditional headpiece of the Osage men dancers, described earlier in chapter 2—and the responsibilities of the dance are explained to the boy by the Dance Chairman.

When a boy is to be introduced to the dance, the Dance Chairman is notified before the I'n-Lon-Schka and makes the arrangements for the ceremony, which occurs during the breaks between the dance sets on a specified day of the I'n-Lon-Schka. At the appropriate time, the boy is presented to the Dance Chairman by his parents and grandparents.[35] The Dance Chairman announces to those assembled that the boy, "John Shaw (Hu-lah Ton-ga)," is to be introduced to the dance. Archie Ma-

Fig. 15. Archie Mason tying on the roach of Charles Tillman III,
a young man being introduced to the dance in the Grayhorse
I'n-Lon-Schka. Charles Tillman, Jr., is the observer.

Fig. 16. Browning Pipestem tying on the roach of John J. Jake,
a young boy being introduced to the dance in the Grayhorse
I'n-Lon-Schka. Note the difference in age between this boy
and the young man in Fig. 15. Observers are Anna K. Roberts,
left, and Kathryn Ann Roberts Jake, right.

son, in tying the roach on John Tallchief at the 1976 Grayhorse
I'n-Lon-Schka, said: "One of our customs is to initiate a young
boy into the dance. This is the first time for John Tallchief, son
of Mr. and Mrs. Harry Tallchief, to take part in our dances. At
this time we place the roach on this boy and wish him all of our
blessings, wherever he goes and dances."[36]

After the roach headpiece is tied on the boy's head, an
eagle feather is placed in the roach last during the ceremony.
This eagle feather has great significance for the Osages. It be-

comes the real symbol of the boy's introduction to the dance. In recent decades the boy usually has remained standing as the roach and eagle feather were placed on his head (Figs. 15 and 16). The old tradition was to seat the boy on a blanket as the feather was placed in the roach, the roach having been tied on the boy's head before he was presented for the ceremony.[37]

A family may choose in which manner the roach and feather are attached. The practice of carrying the roach is to be tied on during the ceremony is a northern Indian tradition used now by most of the Osages in the introduction to the dance.[38] The traditional Osage way was before the ceremony to anchor the roach with a strip of buckskin tied to a piece of braided hair on the top of the boy's head. The hair was braided at the spot measured by the heel of the hand placed at the bridge of the nose and reaching to mid scalp. I watched this process at the 1987 Grayhorse I'n-Lon-Schka as an Osage mother braided a young dancer's top hair and pushed the braid through a hole in the buckskin strip which served as a holder for the roach and feather. In the 1970s and 1980s the roach was anchored by two leather thongs from the roach tied under the chin.

After the roach has been tied on the boy's head and the eagle feather placed in the center of it, gifts are given by the boy's family to dance officials such as the Dance Chairman and Drumkeeper or money is "placed on the drum." Each gift is announced by the Dance Chairman, and the recipient is called forward to be greeted by the boy and his family and to receive his gift. After the presentation of gifts, the boy is officially a part of the I'n-Lon-Schka dances and is led to the dancers' bench of the district to which he belongs. From this point the boys and their families choose the level of commitment to the dance. In time, they may become members of the selected dance organization or simply come to dance and be a part of the I'n-Lon-Schka.[39]

Traditions of Fines and Gifts

An important part of the I'n-Lon-Schka is the tradition of fines and gifts. Fines are levied for violations of rules and regulations, misconduct, and articles dropped on the dance floor.[40] At Grayhorse, much attention is given to fining. At the breaks between the dance sets, the Dance Chairman announces any fines and the reasons for them. Any person being fined is called forward to pay his fine to the proper official. For example, at Grayhorse in the 1974 I'n-Lon-Schka, one of the Tail Dancers— not the host Head Tail Dancer—signaled with his coup stick for a repeat of a chorus, and only the host Head Tail Dancer is allowed to do this. Consequently, the Tail Dancer in error had to pay the host Head Tail Dancer a monetary fine for his mistake.

As noted earlier, any dancer who drops or loses an article of his traditional dress on the dance floor must pay a fine to the Whipman who retrieves it. This is done publicly at the breaks between the dance sets. At Pawhuska, however, the fining is not as public as at Grayhorse, and less attention is given to it. The Pawhuska Dance Chairman instructs his Whipmen simply to bring the man who has been fined to him during the break between the dance sets.[41]

Aside from the gifts that are given by honored individuals, gifts are given to persons for services performed. For example, the Town Crier is given gifts for "calling" an individual's or a family's name. Gifts are also given to substitutes. During the 1975 Grayhorse I'n-Lon-Schka, one of the designated Whipmen was unable to serve in his position because of a broken leg. He gave a gift of a blanket to the man who replaced him in his position. In the 1976 Grayhorse I'n-Lon-Schka another of the designated Whipmen could not participate because of a death in his family, and he, too, gave a gift to the man who replaced him.

Before the Water Boys may drink, they must be given a monetary gift by a family. Upon receiving this gift, they must first go to the Dance Chairman, who announces that they have received a gift from that family. Then they may drink, at Grayhorse crossing each others' dipper arms as they do. All of these gifts are announced by the Dance Chairman at the breaks between the dance sets.

Variations in Traditions among Villages

The observance of the old regulations and rules varies among the three Osage villages, each with its own dance committee, Drumkeeper, and Dance Chairman. This freedom to interpret the old rules for themselves accounts for some of the variations among the three villages, but the two different sources for their I'n-Lon-Schka drums—the Kaws and the Poncas—account for others.

No one is allowed to leave the dance floor at Grayhorse without the permission of the Dance Chairman. This is not observed so strictly at the other two villages. The Water Boys at Grayhorse "water" the singers first and then the dancers, with the next dance set delayed until all of the watering is completed. However, at Pawhuska, in order not to interrupt the dances for too long a period, the singers are instructed by the Dance Chairman to begin as soon as they have been watered and have had a smoke break, even if the dancers have not all been watered. Any dancer who has not been watered and wants water may remain seated on the bench after the dancing has resumed until the water bucket has been brought to him.

Pawhuska and Hominy have allowed the dance organization members to assume some of the old traditional positions; for example, a Whipman in Pawhuska also serves in a dual capacity as the Cedarman. Grayhorse still maintains the traditional single positions. Pawhuska and Hominy have the drum brought in before the dancers, while at Grayhorse, after all of the visiting dancers have been seated, the drum is brought in by the Drum Warmer followed by the Grayhorse dancers.

At a Pawhuska introduction-to-the-dance ceremony, the boy puts on the roach at home and wears it to the dance, and then the eagle feather is added at the dance. The Dance Chairman is the only one to conduct the ceremony at both Hominy and Pawhuska. At Grayhorse the roach and feather are both put on at the dance. The father carries the eagle feather and the mother carries the roach. Both the Dance Chairman and the elders "roach" at Grayhorse.

At Grayhorse the Drumkeeper strikes the drum to open the I'n-Lon-Schka dances each year. At Pawhuska the Drumkeeper strikes the drum to open the I'n-Lon-Schka only if he is new.

At Grayhorse, according to the old tradition, raffles and collections are not allowed as a means of helping with the expenses of the I'n-Lon-Schka. It is felt that the Drumkeeper has assumed this financial burden when he accepts the drum, and if he cannot accept the financial responsibility, he should not accept the drum. However, at Pawhuska and Hominy some raffles and collections are allowed to help defray the I'n-Lon-Schka costs. Benefits during the year are also held by the Dance Chairman, cooks, and other members of the I'n-Lon-Schka dance organizations to help with the expenses at Pawhuska and Hominy. Committee members, district families, and friends are allowed to help by donating rations for the feeding of the visitors and guests in all three villages.

The term *Head Committeeman* is used in Pawhuska, while *Dance Chairman* is used in Grayhorse.

It is the choice of the Drumkeeper, Dance Chairman, and dance organization within each of the villages to decide whether to remain with the old traditions or to incorporate new traditions into the I'n-Lon-Schka. The ceremonies and dances proceed in a dignified manner in spite of the great numbers of dancers and visitors. According to Florence Rheam, "Many of the religious aspects of the I'n-Lon-Schka have disappeared, but not the involved rules which have changed very little over one hundred years. . . . Dances are strictly disciplined and everyone is trained in their meanings."[42]

4. The I'n-Lon-Schka Music

It has been flippantly said that Indian music is the pandemonium of a small boy conducted with the dignity of his grandfather.[1]

The Osage music of the I'n-Lon-Schka, like the I'n-Lon-Schka traditions and dances and the Osage language itself, is handed down by word of mouth from one generation to the next. Although much of Indian cultures has been lost, Indian music has continued to flourish, since Indians have been able to keep their songs when it has been impossible or impractical for them to keep other elements of their tribal life. The music of American Indians is today perhaps the most vital symbol of their cultural and tribal identity.[2]

Because most Indian singing occurs in the open air, the Indians consider the carrying quality of a voice of great importance. Choral singing is preferred to solo singing, with the men singers at dances traditionally seated around a large drum, singing as the drum is beaten. Women in some tribes are often seated a few feet behind the men, often singing an octave higher than the men. A melody may be interrupted at any point by a singer who contributes an improvisation or a traditional contribution such as an imitation of wild animal calls; by singers giving sharp, shrill cries according to their spontaneous emotional feelings; or by women giving their familiar tremolo, a popular notion of which is the war cry created by an Indian warrior's patting his mouth with the flat of his hand as he yells. In fact, Indian women produce the tremolo by fluttering their tongues against the roofs of their mouths as they wail. This sound is referred to as a "lulu," and it is an expression of gratitude produced upon receiving a gift or acknowledging a song is good. In contrast, a man whoops or hollers as an expression of gratitude. Both whoops and lulus are produced by others than the singers.[3]

I heard the tremolo sound during the 1974 and 1975 I'n-Lon-Schka dances, but never located the persons producing it. Then in the summer of 1976 I was seated directly across from a row of Indian women at Grayhorse and observed the sound being made. One of the women occasionally stood, danced quietly in place to the drumbeats, and then produced the cry described above. From her partially opened mouth, without the benefit of her hand patting her mouth, came the tremolo—a high, clear, penetrating warbling sound.

The singing of Indians is accompanied primarily by percussion instruments with different tones for a varied effect but with indefinite pitch. The only exception to these percussion instruments is the occasional use of small wood or bone flutes. The percussion instruments are simple, with the most common rhythm instrument being the drum, which, though it is found in varying sizes, is ordinarily about the size of a snare drum. The drums are made from a dried animal skin stretched over a hollowed hickory log or other cylindrical frame of wood. They have either one or two heads, with the larger drums supported by drum racks. Other percussion instruments are rattles made of rawhide and filled with pebbles or the dew claws of deer and bells worn by the dancers around their waists, ankles, or knees.[4]

The rhythm of Indian songs is characterized by heavy accents occurring at irregular intervals and with measures of varying lengths. The Indians keep the rhythms of a song as he or she learned them. Often the Indian singer-drummer carries two different rhythm patterns simultaneously, one with the voice and the other with the drum. On long notes the singers often continue the rhythmic beats even after the drum has stopped.[5]

The Indian singer's tone production, both men's and women's, may be described in such terms as tense, harsh, raucous, tight, and nasal with a light, clear falsetto and a fast, narrow vibrato. The vibrato is both cultivated and admired. There is much slurring from one melodic tone to another. The tones seem to be forced outward by an action of the throat muscles which gives the tone its carrying power. The teeth are slightly separated with little change in the positions of the lips.[6]

Song melodies characteristically descend, covering large

ranges. Singers begin high, sometimes in a falsetto voice, and descend to a growling depth. Sometimes the song will ascend in the middle and then descend again, but the most apparent characteristic of Indian songs is a steadily descending melody from beginning to end. Often in songs with this steady downward trend, the final note is not the keynote.[7]

The most frequent intervals found in Indian melodies are the major seconds and minor thirds. One of the most important figural groupings is the span of a fourth, including intervals of a minor third and a major second, shown in Musical Example 1. Most melodies are based on only a few tones with two very common groupings being (1) *cdega,* without the fourth and seventh scale degrees, and (2) *acdeg,* without the second and sixth scale degrees.[8]

Men are the most active singers, since they are believed to have special powers that women do not have. As shamans, priests, and medicine men, they treat the sick with song and sacred rituals. To be a good singer a man must have a large repertoire of songs, an accurate memory, and an understanding of the meaning and special purpose of each song. Often a class of expert singers will develop in a tribe. Although they do not earn a living from singing, they are respected for their ability to sing well.[9]

Although each tribe has special song writers, any member of the tribe may create a song descriptive of some event or outstanding achievement. Mathews relates a story about a typical impromptu composition of a song by a young Osage. After a skirmish with the Pawnees, a young Osage warrior who had successfully counted coup on a leading Pawnee brave asked a friend who had seen his coup touch to go ahead of him into camp and have a song about his successful coup ready to greet

Music Example 1. Common intervals found in American Indian melodies.

him upon his arrival in camp. As the young brave rode into camp, his friend sang a fine warrior song describing the successful coup.[10]

The ethnomusicological term *conscious composition* applies to these songs commissioned by members of the tribe and created by the Indian songmakers for special events. Other songs, such as those received in dreams, are created by *unconscious composition*. These songs are believed to have magic power.

Songs may be owned. Some songs are inherited in families, and the original ownership of a song is respected by Indians some generations later, with the name of the owner mentioned as the song is sung.[11]

Some Indian songs are composed with words, while others are not. In the songs which do not have words, nonsense syllables, or vocables—syllables having the most singable vowel sounds—are used. Songs with words most often honor the dead, brave war deeds, the success of a hunter, or the mysterious and secret rituals of the shamans. Some songs remain unchanged, while others are revised each year. If songs are sung as a part of a religious celebration, the singers must sing only the appropriate songs and these only in the proper order, or the ceremony will go unheeded by the Great Spirit. In family songs it was often the custom to add a new name to an old song, and this was a compliment to the named person since it implied that a living man had distinguished himself as greatly as the heroes of the past named in the song. When such a song is sung, the man is expected to rise and dance alone and to give gifts to the singers or to the company.[12]

The music of the Osage I'n-Lon-Schka is primarily vocal music, accompanied by the rhythmic beats of a drum and the knee bells of the dancers. Occasional cries, tremelos, and pipings on small wooden flutes punctuate the songs at any point as the spirit moves the individual dancer, singer, or tribesman. The vocal music is provided by a chorus of men singing in unison, who are sometimes joined by a smaller chorus of women singers singing an octave higher in unison. The men, serving as both the singers and the drummers, are seated around a large drum in the center of the dance arbor. The women are seated in a circle directly around the men's circle. The drumbeats are struck in perfect unison by the singers-drummers, who average from fifteen to twenty men in the circle. The drumbeats are steady, even-paced, and unchanging in rhythm values but changing from light to heavy beats upon occasion.

The Osage singing is high-pitched—in both the men's and women's voices—with an unusual tone quality which lacks resonance but which has a clarity and purity of tone and pitch. There is an openness to the musical sound created by the vocal tone quality, as well as by the unison singing of the men and the occasional paralleling of the melody by the women an octave higher. Both the tone quality and the unison singing enable these melodies to carry well, even above the heavy drumbeats and pipings, the town crier's calls, the crowd sounds, and the jingling of some three hundred dancers' knee bells.

Musical Instruments

The instruments of the Osage I'n-Lon-Schka are typical of those used in Indian ceremonials throughout the United States. The most important instrument is the drum, for, as has been noted, it is the instrument through which the Osages communicate with the Great Spirit, Wah'Kon-Tah, and with fellow tribesmen.

The drum used in the I'n-Lon-Schka is made from cowhide stretched over each end of a hollow cylindrical object, usually a round wooden barrel of hickory wood (Fig. 12). The two-foot-long drumsticks of the singers-drummers are wooden shafts with leather or rawhide heads. Each singer-drummer must furnish his own drumsticks. The heating of the drum in order to produce a good, resonant tone, is, as mentioned earlier, the responsibility of the Drum Warmer, who traditionally warms it over a wood fire the morning before an afternoon dance. Even on the hottest days the Drum Warmer heats the drum over a wood fire.

Other instruments used in the Osage I'n-Lon-Schka are the knee bells of the dancers and small wooden flutes. The small flute is usually made from wood or bone and has a high piping sound which is said to imitate the cry of an eagle. At the 1974 I'n-Lon-Schka one very old dancer, a visiting Pawnee, played his flute at each corner of the dance arbor. The significance of his actions is unknown to me.

The knee bells probably came into use by the Osages after
contact had been made with the Europeans. Mathews refers to
these bells as European hawking bells. Before the bells were introduced, rattles made from terrapin shells filled with cougar
teeth probably were used to add to the sounds of a dance. Osages
also used deer "toes" (toenails) as their traditional noisemakers
before the bells. Some Osages still wear these deer "toes" in
powwows, but the bells are considered the proper noisemakers
in the I'n-Lon-Schka today.[13]

The Osages regularly wear bells around their knees as a
part of their traditional dress. Originally the Osages must have
attached some significance to the numbers of bells worn by the
individual dancer, but that significance is lost today, when all
the dancers wear bells for both their sound and their decorative
qualities without special regard to number. Different sound
effects are created by the bells in the dances when the step
changes. For example, during the trot songs the step changes to
a one-step or flat-foot trot step (described in chapter 5) instead
of the typical toe-heel step of most of the dances. The sounds of
the bells change from the accented ching-CHING, ching-CHING of
the toe-heel step to the even ching, ching, ching of the one-step.

Analysis of the Songs

In the Osage I'n-Lon-Schka most of the songs have descending melodic lines, many stepwise progressions of major
seconds with some skips of minor thirds and occasional skips of
perfect fourths and fifths.[14] There are numerous repetitions of
the melodic phrases with many sequential melodic motives.
The forms of the songs are very simple, usually in two parts
with the second part being similar to or a variation of the first.
These parts—usually considered verse and chorus—may be repeated at the discretion or desire of the Head Singer, a lead
singer, or the host Head Tail Dancer, often extending the length
of a song greatly. Although the melodies at first seem to sound
alike to the untutored ear, on repeated and careful hearings different melodic and rhythmic patterns begin to be apparent.
Rarely is a song repeated during the four days of the I'n-Lon-
Schka, and it is not unusual for some two hundred different
songs to be sung during the ceremonies.

The Franklin Shaw Individual Song transcribed in Music Example 2 is a typical Indian melody. Each phrase, with the exception of the first part of phrase *F,* has a steady downward trend. The most common intervals are major seconds. There are very few skips except the few minor thirds, several perfect fourths, and the wide leaps between repeats such as the skip of an eleventh at the end of phrase *E* and the beginning of phrase *F* and the leap of a twelfth between phrases *H* and *A.* There is much repetition and similarity in melodic motives throughout the song. Although the song begins on F above middle C, the prominent tone is E-flat. The first two phrases center around E-flat tonally, and the cadences end on E-flat and B-flat, the dominant of E-flat. The final tone is B-flat and, as is typical in many Indian melodies, the final note in this song is not the keynote. The tonal grouping for this song is E-flat, F, G, B-flat, and C. This is the tonal grouping without the fourth and seventh scale degrees. The range of the Franklin Shaw Individual Song is typical of the wide range of many of the Indian songs. It is shown in Musical Example 3.

Phrase analysis of the Franklin Shaw Individual Song is as follows: Phrase *A* begins on F and moves stepwise in major seconds downward except for one upward step. Phrase *B* begins on F but centers around E-flat and moves in major seconds and minor thirds in a descending movement to B-flat below middle C. Phrase *C* is an exact repetition of phrase B. Phrase *D* is a repetition of phrase *A* one octave lower; this phrase is linked to phrase *C* by the B-flat and skip of a perfect fourth to F. Phrase *E* is a repetition of Phrase *B* one octave lower with an extended cadence note. Phrase *F* is a different melodic phrase with skips of a perfect fourth between E-flat and B-flat in the first of the phrase, then descending major seconds with one minor third skip. Phrase *G* is a repetition of phrase *D*. Phrase *H* is a repetition of phrase *B,* two octaves lower.

The Beginning Song of the 1976 I'n-Lon-Schka at Grayhorse, Hominy, and Pawhuska is transcribed in Music Example 4. Analysis of the Beginning Song shows its range to be similar to that of the Franklin Shaw Individual Song and reflects the wide range typical of many Indian songs. The Beginning Song range is shown in Musical Example 5.

The common intervals appearing in Indian music of the major

Music Example 2. The Franklin Shaw Individual Song,
transcribed by Alice Anne Callahan.

Music Example 3. Range of the Franklin Shaw Individual Song.

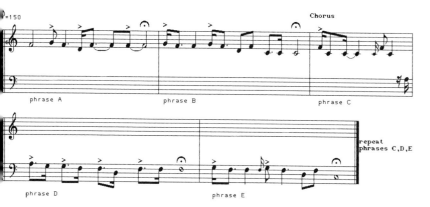

Music Example 4. The Beginning Song at Grayhorse, Hominy and
Pawhuska, transcribed by Alice Anne Callahan.

Music Example 5. Range of the Beginning Song.

second and minor third appear frequently in this Beginning Song. The melodic line descends, but not as steadily as does the Franklin Shaw Individual Song. The tonal grouping for this song is F, G, A, C, D. This, like the Shaw song, falls into the grouping without the fourth and seventh scale degrees. The prominent tone is F, with this song beginning on F and the first two phrases centering around F. The cadence points are on F and C, the dominant of F. The final note is C, but like the Shaw song and other Indian songs with a downward trend, the last note is not the keynote.

Phrase analysis of the Beginning Song is as follows: Phrase *A* begins on F, moves upward and downward in major seconds and minor thirds, and ends on F. Phrase *B* begins on F and is very similar to phrase *A* but moves on down to the dominant C for the cadence note. Phrase *C* has skips of perfect fourths up and down between tones F and C and ends on C. Phrase *D* be-

Music Example 6. The Hunk-A-Hoppy Individual Song excerpt, transcribed by Alice Anne Callahan.

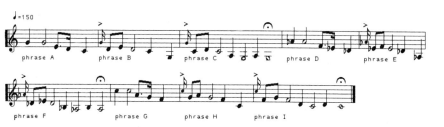

Music Example 7. The Thomas Joe Lane Individual Song
excerpt, transcribed by Alice Anne Callahan.

gins on A and descends stepwise in major seconds with skips of
a minor third at the cadence point, which is F. Phrase *E* is a repetition of phrase *B* an octave lower and with the cadence tone C
extended. Phrases *F, G,* and *H* are an exact repetition of phrases
C, D, and *E.*

Excerpts of the Hunk-A-Hoppy and Thomas Joe Lane individual songs appear in Musical Examples 6 and 7, respectively.
Both songs have traditional tonal groupings and melodic intervals. In both there are sharper accents on the grace notes or six-
teenth notes. As the verse or chorus of each song is repeated, it
ascends instead of descending, with both songs ending on a
much higher pitch than that on which they begin. Both songs,
especially the Thomas Joe Lane Song, have more skips of perfect fourths and fifths than the Franklin Shaw Individual Song
and Beginning Song have. Because I was unable to transcribe
the Hunk-A-Hoppy and Lane songs as completely as the Shaw
and Beginning songs, the phrase-by-phrase analysis is omitted.
In all of these songs I have transcribed, the melodic rhythms
proved to be the most difficult to transcribe with accuracy.

Rhythm and Tempo

The most readily apparent characteristic of the Osage I'n-
Lon-Schka music is the steady, driving drumbeat produced by
the singers-drummers, some fifteen to twenty men, who sound
as if they are but one drummer. The steady Osage drum rhythms
have virtually none of the complex polyrhythms, improvisatory
passages, and sophistication of African or Polynesian drum mu-

sic and seem to serve a much more limited purpose, that of simply accompanying the progress of the songs and providing cues to the dancers. The drumbeats are either light or heavy with no intermediate dynamic levels, and are not used in the duple- and triple-meter patterns so common to traditional Western music.[15]

The patterns of heavy drumbeats serve as cues for repeated verses; choruses; type of song, such as the war songs; and stopping points. In the following drumbeat patterns the heavy beats signal the end of the verse, chorus, or close of the song. Almost every Tail Dance concludes with five heavy drumbeats. It is an embarrassment to any Tail Dancer who does not end precisely on the final drumbeat. In recent years the person leading the song, whether the Head Singer or a lead singer, cues with his hand for the heavy and light drumbeats, repeats, or fading out of a song because of the new singers around the drum and their unfamiliarity with the songs. In earlier times the hand cues were unnecessary, as the older singers knew the songs and instinctively knew the appropriate times for the heavy and light drumbeats.

The following examples of the drumbeat patterns are from the first three songs of the 1976 Grayhorse I'n-Lon-Schka Saturday evening dance as I recorded them. The · represents the light beat and the - represents the heavy beat.

First Song or Beginning Song ($\flat$ = 150):

```
··································································· ····
··········································· ···············_·_·_·············
·····································································
·······································_·_·_·············_·_·_··········
······························ _ _ _ _ _ / / ····················
·········· _ _ _ _ _
```

Second Song ($\flat$ = 160–176):

```
·······················································_·_·_··· 
·····································································
····_·_·_·····················_·_·_ - - - - - - - - - - - -
- - - - - - - - - - - - - - - - - - - - - - - ·_·_·············_·_·_
- - - - - - - - - - - - - - - - - - - - - - - - - - - - - / /
```
(approximately a twenty-second break) Tail Dance ··············
··········· _ _ _ _ (three-second break before the next dance)

Third Song (♪ = 160–184):

```
· · · · · · · · · · · · · · · · · · · · · · · · · · · · · · · · · · · · · - · - · - · · · · · · · · · · · · · · · · ·
· · · · · - · - · - - - - - - - - - - - - - - - - - - - - - - - - - - - - - - - - - - - - -
- - - - - - - - - - - - - - - · - - - - - - - - · - · - · · · · · · · · · · · · - - - - - - - -
- - - - - - - - - - - - - - - - - - - - - - - - - - - - - - - - - - - - - - - - - - - - - -
- · - · · · · · · · · · · · · · · · · · · · - · - - - - - - - - - - Tail Dance · · · · · · · · · ·
· · · · · · · · · · · · · · · · · · - - - - - (A three-second break before the next
```
dance)

In all of the I'n-Lon-Schka songs the - · - · - · drum pattern indicates a repeat of a verse in which the drumbeat remains light. The pattern of - · - · usually precedes a section of heavy drumbeats. All of the Tail Dances end with the five heavy drumbeats.

In the songs of the I'n-Lon-Schka there is a near-continuous flow of either the drumbeats or the voices within a group of songs referred to as a set. Either the voices or the drumbeats resume their performance almost immediately after a break, creating a smoothness and flow of sounds within a set and linking them together as a group. There is a brief break after each song before the Tail Dance following it. This break is approximately twenty seconds long to allow the dance floor to clear quickly before the Tail Dancers perform the Tail Dance. Following the Tail Dance there is only a brief three-second pause to allow the Tail Dancers to leave the dance floor before the next song begins. Usually the drumbeats begin before the voices, but occasionally the voices lead off.

A change of tempo occurs from the slower-paced beginning songs to the faster-paced songs in the middle and at the end of a dance. Quite often there is a change of tempo within one song. Metronome indications for the songs cited above indicate the tempo differences between the songs as well as the tempo changes within one song. In most songs, the tempo increases as the drumbeats become heavy and as the choruses are repeated. The fastest tempos are reserved for the Warrior and War songs performed toward the end of the Saturday night dances. The tempos of these songs not only begin at a very fast pace but also increase dramatically in the course of the song, creating much tension and excitement not only among the dancers but also among the listeners and observers. The Warrior and War songs are introduced by loud, sharply accented drumbeats interspersed between steady, light beats imitating gunshots. The metronome beats begin at ♪ = 192 and increase in tempo up to ♪ = 240 or 280. The Head Singer must be especially sensitive to the correct tempos and to the appropriate times for an increase or decrease in the tempo in order to achieve the right spirit for the I'n-Lon-Schka. This careful attention to pacing is evident throughout the four days of the ceremonies.

While the drumbeat remains steady, unwavering, and without rhythmic variety, the melodic rhythms of the singers prove to be much more interesting and complex. There is great rhythmic variety and irregularity in the melodies of the songs. Often there is a difference between the drumbeat and the melodic beat of the singers, with a tension created between them in the unexpected accents and syncopations of the melodies. The steady drumbeats act as a backdrop to these irregular melodic rhythms.

Musical Examples 8, 9, 10, 11, and 12 demonstrate the

Music Example 8. Melodic rhythm patterns in a 1914 Osage Song of Triumph, transcribed by Alice Fletcher.

Music Example 9. Melodic rhythm patterns in a 1914 Osage Song of Triumph, transcribed by Alice Fletcher.

Music Example 10. Melodic rhythm patterns in the Franklin Shaw Individual Song, transcribed by Alice Anne Callahan from a tape of Morris Lookout made in August, 1975.

Music Example 11. Melodic rhythm patterns in the Beginning Song, transcribed by Alice Anne Callahan.

Music Example 12. Melodic rhythmic patterns in the Trot Song, transcribed by Alice Ann Callahan.

complexity of the melodic rhythms of the Osage songs. Examples 8 and 9, with similar rhythmic patterns, were transcribed by Alice Fletcher in 1914.[16] Her transcriptions have been divided into the traditional measures, but I have thought it wiser to leave my own transcriptions, in Musical Examples 10, 11, and 12, without bar lines. Note the regularity of the rhythms as well as the accents in the Trot Song in Musical Example 12 compared with Musical Examples 8 through 11.

The I'n-Lon-Schka Songs

William K. Powers wrote, "The song was always the most important part of the ceremony, usually more important than the dance."[17] Songs serve a religious purpose for the Indian, and the music is believed to be endowed with mystical powers.

The cultural interchange between the Osages and other American Indian tribes relocated in reservation lands was far-reaching. Many of the songs, as well as the traditions, of the I'n-Lon-Schka came to the Osages from the Ponca and Kaw tribes. Once these songs had been given to the Osages, they became Osage songs, and the Kaws and Poncas no longer used them. Today the Poncas remain noted as both singers and composers and compose many of the new family and individual songs for the Osages.

Each afternoon and evening dance of the first three days of the I'n-Lon-Schka is divided into sets. Each Thursday and Friday evening set contains six to eight songs. In both afternoon and evening dances, the first set opens with the Beginning Song, to which no one dances. The Beginning Song is followed by six or seven other songs before the first water and smoke break. The second set has from six to eight songs. At the conclusion of the second set, and at the discretion of the Dance Chairman, the afternoon dance usually stops.[18] During an evening dance there are usually three sets, with water and smoke breaks between; each set lasts about thirty minutes. On Saturday evening there are usually four sets with some ten to twelve songs in a set. The singers-drummers may repeat a favorite song as many as six times. As a result of the repeated songs and extended sets, the Saturday night dance is longer than those of the previous two evenings.

Although most Osage songs can claim single authorship, there are some that are the product of two or three composers. Morris Lookout writes or composes songs only for those persons for whom he is inspired to write.[19] The Franklin Shaw Individual Song, discussed earlier in this chapter, was written by Wakon Iron and falls into the "conscious composition" category, among the commissioned songs praising a man's success or generosity. Iron received from Franklin Shaw's son, John, a palomino horse in appreciation for the Shaw Individual Song.

Some Indians have visions and receive songs in their dreams. One Osage Indian whose song came to him in a dream, dreamed that he was standing before a grave. There came a blinding light and a voice saying to him that the grave was also the way of life, and that life was infinite, even beyond death. The song he sang told of this message from his dream.[20]

The I'n-Lon-Schka songs are strophic and vary from those with vocables but no words through those with few words to those with words throughout. In some old songs in which the words have been lost, vocables are used to prevent the original melody from being lost. Many of the afternoon songs are without words, or are with only a few words, and are considered preliminary or preparatory songs to the evening dances. Some songs have words only in the chorus and vocables in the verse section. Many of the family songs have vocables in the verse section and the words for the family or individual in the chorus. There are those few songs that have words in both chorus and verse. Many of the words are rearranged or divided to make a better rhyme or to conform to the melody. Although most of the songs sung in the I'n-Lon-Schka in the 1970s and 1980s are still in the Ponca language, there are plans to include a number of songs in the old Osage language in the future.[21]

In the I'n-Lon-Schka of the 1880s the songs were in a particular order or sequence. A leader—with the Osage title of *ho'kah*—was responsible for seeing that the songs were sung in the correct order. If a mistake was made, the song sequence had to begin again. Today the title *ho'kah* is sometimes used in referring to the main singers who have been through the ranks successfully and understand the songs and the spirit of the I'n-Lon-Schka music. The precise order of the songs in the 1880s is no longer known, but the currently observed order is believed to be similar to the original.[22]

The I'n-Lon-Schka Song Categories

The songs of the I'n-Lon-Schka are grouped into different categories such as prayer songs, warrior songs, calling songs, and family songs. They are not known by individual titles except in the case of the family songs.[23] There are some new songs "on the drum," but 75 percent of the I'n-Lon-Schka songs sung in the mid-1970s have been handed down. Some of these songs once belonged to old families in the Osage tribe who released them for use in the I'n-Lon-Schka. Regardless of their category and subject, all of these songs are sacred in that they express the Osage religion and belief in a higher power.[24]

There are certain I'n-Lon-Schka songs that are considered to be classics, and they are saved for the Friday and Saturday evening dances in the later part of the dances. These songs have words and special meaning for the Osage and like all dance ceremony songs are sacred in that they express some aspect of Osage religious belief. The Head Singer must know the appropriate time for their inclusion in a dance. The subject of these songs is often death. An Osage does not fear death, and many of these classic songs express the belief that it is an honor to die. Such songs are the trot songs, which are the only songs in the I'n-Lon-Schka that are not allowed to be performed in the powwows.

The trot songs originally came from an old Osage ceremony of mourning which is no longer performed. This ceremony was a celebration of death and was lost in the late nineteenth and early twentieth centuries when the whites had to a large extent Christianized the Osages. In this celebration of death the Osages, dressed in their traditional dress, each with a horse and standing four abreast, would dance in place as they sang the trot songs. The horses also danced and trotted. Very few singers are given the right to sing these trot songs. Only sixteen of the songs survive in private Osage collections, and they are all supposed to be sung together as a unit. Today, usually four of them are performed late in the Saturday night I'n-Lon-Schka without the horses but with the dancers lined up four abreast and circling to imitate the horses.[25] The trot songs are characterized by more regular melodic rhythms, as described in the rhythm transcription earlier in this chapter; moderate tempo; and a change of dance step and bell accents.

In the afternoons the singers-drummers sing the songs that are referred to as the calling songs—calling the tribesmen together. These songs are simple, with few words, and are considered introductory songs. One of the calling songs is the Beginning Song of each afternoon and evening dance, to which no

one dances. I noticed in 1976 that the same Beginning Song, transcribed in Music Example 4 in this chapter, was used in the Grayhorse, Pawhuska, and Hominy dances. It is slower paced than the songs appearing later in the dance. The younger singers-drummers have difficulty in learning these calling songs because they are not as interesting as the warrior, prayer, and trot songs. In the text the words "I'n-Lon-Schka dom'bah-hah has'kah-hoo" appear. These words make reference to the I'n-Lon-Schka and pay tribute to the ideals symbolized by this dance.[26]

Warrior songs are in praise or tribute to an individual who has counted coup and are usually performed late in an evening dance. These narrative songs tell of the deeds of great warriors—even enemy warriors—who have exemplified themselves in battle and war. These songs are characterized by sharp, accented drumbeats that explode unexpectedly from the drummers' circle and signal a faster tempo for the dancers. These songs of triumph and victory direct the thoughts of the men of the tribe to that unseen source of all power which enables human beings to act their part in life.

Prayer songs are heavily spiritual and make reference to the Great Spirit and pay homage to Him. Again expressed in these songs is the Osage recognition of a greater power than oneself. These songs make many references to the I'n-Lon-Schka—the high standards of conduct of the I'n-Lon-Schka, the difficulties in living up to the I'n-Lon-Schka. The expression, "I'n-Lon-Schka gah," is often heard in these prayer songs. Translated literally, this means, "The I'n-Lon-Schka is making it" and indicates that everything the Osage participants are doing is being done with the proper protocol, respect, and dignity.

The individual and family songs are sung on the afternoon of the fourth day of the I'n-Lon-Schka—Sunday. There continues to be a great deal of pride and attention given to the ownership of these individual songs in the 1970s and 1980s, with the Dance Chairman often announcing the ownership or inheritance of certain songs before they are sung. These songs honor and recount the deeds of the great leaders within the Osage tribe, both living and dead. Most of the individual songs are for persons who have displayed leadership, both in the tribe and in society, or for those who have shown valor in battle.

Sometimes when an old song is inherited by a younger member in a family, the inheritor may have his name inserted in the song, replacing the name of the older family member.

A line-by-line translation of the text of the Wah'We-See Individual Song composed by Lookout is as follows:[27]

Wah-Sha'She zon-hi dom'bah-nah (Wah-Sha'She zon-hi addresses the Osage people courteously; dom'bah-nah asks them to give their attention to the individual for whom the song is composed).

Wah'We-See ska-xhe (Wah'We-See is the individual's Indian name, meaning "Buffalo Jumping over Wallow"; ska-xhe indicates that the individual is conducting himself according to the ideals of the I'n-Lon-Schka).

Dough-dah hun'kah (dough-dah hun'kah is the name for the Dance Committeemen and calls for their attention as principals of the I'n-Lon-Schka).

I'n-Lon-Schka kah-xhe (kah-xhe refers to the elders or old people who have taught the I'n-Lon-Schka ideals).

Wah-Sha'She zon-hi dom'bah-nah (a repeat of line one).

Wah'We-See wah-sho'shay (Wah'We-See is the individual's name repeated, as is common in these individual songs; wah-sho'shay indicates that he has exemplified himself in combat, drawing blood from the enemy, and is entitled to be called a warrior).

A literal translation of the text of the ceremonial songs conveys little of the meaning of the song to an outsider. The imagery is personal, symbolic, and sometimes mystical, and has no close counterpart in Western music. Further, the text cannot be considered or understood outside of the elaborate ritual, tribal beliefs, and traditions of which it is a part. A "translation" of I'n-Lon-Schka songs into meaningful English is not possible in the way that a German or Russian song can be translated into English.

When a song has been composed for an individual, a member of his family goes to the I'n-Lon-Schka dance organization in that particular village and informs them that a song "has been made for my father." The I'n-Lon-Schka dance organization decides whether the song will be a part of the I'n-Lon-Schka and whether the I'n-Lon-Schka will accept it "for the drum." If approved, the new song will be sung on Sunday afternoon each year in that village whether the person for whom the song was composed or his family is there or not. Once a song is approved, it "belongs to the drum." A person can remove his individual or family song "from the drum" only with the greatest difficulty. A person wishing to remove his individual song must meet again with the dance organization in his village and explain his reasons for removing the song. If the request to remove the song is denied, the song "remains on the drum." Once it has been "taken off the drum," it can never go back on.

The program of the family songs begins with the Drumkeeper's Song. This is a traditional song for the Drumkeeper, and not a new song for the Drumkeeper. The second song is the traditional song for the Dance Chairman and committeemen. Following this song are the individual and family songs—some twenty-four in the 1974 Grayhorse I'n-Lon-Schka. Often the third and fourth songs are ones written specifically for the current Drumkeeper and Dance Chairman. If these men remain leaders in the tribe, their songs remain on the drum long after they have served their respective offices. After all the individual songs have been sung, the I'n-Lon-Schka is concluded with the singing of the Whipmen's Song, the Cooks' Song, and the Lady Singers' Song. These last songs are optional. Included in Appendix C is a list of the family songs in the 1975 Grayhorse I'n-Lon-Schka.

In the summers of 1974, 1975, and 1976 in which I heard the family and individual songs sung at Grayhorse and Pawhuska, I noticed that certain familiar family names kept recurring and also that a few new names were added, such as the new individual song at Grayhorse in 1976 for Thomas Joe Lane. After hearing a recording of the 1967 Grayhorse family and individual songs, I discovered that many of the same family songs were still present on the 1976 Grayhorse drum. As examples of the continuity and longevity of these family and individual songs, I list below, by the name of the individual honored, those songs from the 1967 I'n-Lon-Schka that also appeared on the drum in the 1976 Grayhorse I'n-Lon-Schka.[28]

Johnny Williams in 1967 was the Grayhorse Drumkeeper and had a special individual song composed for him. In 1976,

Dance Chairman Browning Pipestem spoke for John's mother, saying that this young man was serving where there were few doctors and little medical services available.

Archie Mason in 1967 was the Grayhorse Dance Chairman for the I'n-Lon-Schka. He remained until 1974 in that office and then served as an advisor for the Grayhorse district.

Victor Akers is the subject of one of the older individual songs at Grayhorse. This song was given to Victor Akers by his grandmother Eva Little Star. It had first belonged to his grandfather, who was one of the earlier Grayhorse I'n-Lon-Schka committeemen.

Francis Pipestem, now deceased, was chief of the Oto tribe in 1967 and was married to Rose Pipestem, an Osage. He was very active on the Grayhorse I'n-Lon-Schka dance organization and in the Osage tribe. His son, Browning Pipestem, was chosen to be the Dance Chairman at Grayhorse in 1975.

Wilson Kirk, now deceased, was the father of Rose Pipestem and Charles Kirk, who were both very active in the 1970s Grayhorse I'n-Lon-Schkas. Wilson Kirk was one of the first to participate in a Grayhorse I'n-Lon-Schka dance organization. He was an elder of the tribe and highly respected.

Joe Mason, now deceased, was father of Archie Mason, who was very active in the 1970s and 1980s Grayhorse I'n-Lon-Schkas. Joe Mason was a World War I veteran and an elder in the tribe. He was an active leader in the Grayhorse district during his lifetime.

Mike Watson, now deceased, was active in both the Grayhorse and Pawhuska dance organizations and served as Dance Chairman at one time in Grayhorse. His song says, "Come on, friend, let's dance." This song was one of the older Osage songs surviving from the Kansas days.

Hunk-A-Hoppy was an Osage who died many years ago and was one of the first to have a song on the drum in the Grayhorse district after the Osages moved to Oklahoma. (Transcribed excerpts are in Music Example 6.) This song, too, was one of the old Osage songs surviving from the Kansas days. It says that Hunk-A-Hoppy is a leader's son and that it is difficult to be a leader. The Dance Chairman of the 1975 I'n-Lon-Schka announced that Hunk-A-Hoppy was Gertrude Sroufe's grandfather and that his song was one of the original ones on the Grayhorse drum. To honor this song she gave many gifts.

Henry Tallchief, now deceased, was at one time a very active leader in the Grayhorse district. His song says, "Look at me, I'm treading the tough trail of life."

Franklin Shaw, now deceased, was at one time the assistant chief to Chief Fred Lookout and the acting chief for a short period after the death of Chief Lookout. Shaw was active in the Grayhorse I'n-Lon-Schka dance organization and in the Osage tribe. His son, John Shaw, was one of the Grayhorse dance committeemen for many years and commissioned Mr. Wakon Iron to write his father's song. This song is in the Osage language. (See Music Example 2. A recording of this song has been made.)[29]

The text of the Franklin Shaw Individual Song is as follows:

Hu-Lah Ts'A-Ge Non-Zhin (Hu-Lah Ts'A-Ge is Franklin Shaw's Indian name, meaning "Old Eagle." The term *old* is used here as a term of respect and honor and not necessarily to indicate age. When a man reaches a point in his life at which he has a sense of the customs and traditions and has become one of the leaders, then the term *old* is applied as a way of honoring him. *Non-zhin* literally means "to stand up." This indicates that homage is being paid to an individual for the valuable things that he has given to the tribe, such as his time and talents. The individual's Indian name followed by *non-zhin* appears at the beginning of the chorus of the song. Hu-Lah Ton-Ga is John Shaw's Indian name, meaning "Big Eagle," and will appear in this song sometimes. Note that Hu-Lah Ton-Ga was used in the recording of this song on the tape).

Hon-ba the'tho we-gi see-tha (hon-ba-the'tho means each day you come to me for the goodness you express; we-gi see-tha expresses an appreciation for what the ancestors have left).[30]

The Thomas Joe Lane Individual Song was new in 1976 and was accepted by the Grayhorse I'n-Lon-Schka dance organization for the drum. (Transcribed excerpts are in Music Example 7.) Thomas Joe Lane, a young man, had been active in the Grayhorse dances in previous years and had died tragically in 1975 during the Grayhorse I'n-Lon-Schka. He had been in the Army, had been absent without leave, and was awaiting shipment back to his camp when he committed suicide in the Pawhuska, Oklahoma, jail. Word of his death reached the Grayhorse camp late Friday afternoon of the I'n-Lon-Schka, and a pall was cast over the entire weekend. His grandmother was second cook on the Grayhorse committee, and his family and he were well known in the Grayhorse community. On Sunday afternoon, June 6, 1976, exactly one year after his death, the song was placed on the Grayhorse drum for him. The entire group of dancers joined in his dance, with the visiting tribes standing in place and dancing to the drumbeat to show their respect for the song. Women gave the traditional tremolo and mourning wails during the song. At the end of the dance, the family of Thomas Joe Lane thanked the people who had danced to his song and gave gifts to the many people who had supported them in their grief throughout the year. This was one of the most moving scenes in the I'n-Lon-Schka that I have witnessed. It demonstrated for me again the community feeling and support that the Osages, as well as the visiting tribes, had given to this family—typical of the support that they give to one another.

5. The I'n-Lon-Schka Dance

The I'n-Lon-Schka is a ceremonial dancing style, sometimes referred to by the popular term *straight dance.*
This designation is used in contrast to the term *fancy dance,* the
popular name given to the powwow dancing style. The ceremonial dancing style is dignified, controlled, and reserved, with
the same movements being repeated over and over again. A
basic step chosen by each dancer is repeated or maintained
throughout the straight dance, with most of the movement
being in the head, arms, shoulders, or torso. In contrast to the
sedate straight dance style, the fancy dance involves fast and
difficult footwork and dramatic body movements. In the straight
or ceremonial dancing the emphasis is not on the dancing itself
as much as it is on the total experience of music, dance, ceremony, and colorful traditional dress. The spectators at the ceremonial dances are in harmony with what the dancers, singers,
and members of the dance organization are doing and understand the purpose of the ceremonial dance. This audience sits
quietly, treating the occasion as they would a serious religious
ceremony, without the applause and audience response that are
a part of the powwow.

Archie Mason, Jr., refers to the dancers joining "the joyous
discipline of the dance. . . . It's a joyous time, yet it's a disciplined joyous time for those that participate . . . a very cere-
monious thing with participants receiving a spiritual lift from
that whole experience." Jamake Highwater says, "The steps of
the Indian ceremonial dances are executed with inner grace and
simplicity. . . . It is the deep involvement of the Dancers in the
dance that is the source of magic, not the complexity of the motions." Ed Red Eagle says that in the Osage I'n-Lon-Schka the
dancers are unaware of the spectators as they dance, and are not
dancing for an audience but for themselves. They receive a spir-

itual strength in the dancing around the drum, with the spirit
coming out of both the drum and songs.[1]

As best we know, there has been little change in the dancing style of the I'n-Lon-Schka since the Osages began it. These
dances "go off the same way each year with the same dancing
style and organization of the dances."[2] As already noted, an
evening of the I'n-Lon-Schka dances should end as the dancing
"gets good," in contrast to the powwow dances, which would
continue on into the night if the dancing were "good."[3] Many
tribes, because of their lack of economic independence, charge
admission fees and are compelled to perform the powwow-
style dances to satisfy public demand for this more spectacular,
crowd-pleasing fancy dancing. Because of the Osages' economic independence, they have not needed subsidy and have
not submitted to public pressure for more fancy dancing. One
observer stated, "Their [the Osages'] traditional dance which
they perform annually is never commercialized and retains the
ancient dignity free from powwow histrionics."[4] This same
economic independence has allowed the Osages to maintain
their expensive traditional costumes, which are described in
chapter 6. The I'n-Lon-Schka is one of the few authentic ceremonial dances remaining in the United States today.

Historically, Indian ceremonial dancing has always been a
man's dance, with the movements reflecting and expressing
masculine characteristics.[5] They were men's dances because of
the Indian belief that men had greater power than women in
bringing about the magic associated with music and dance and
because many of the Indian tribes in the past were divided into
warrior societies in which the ceremonial dancing was restricted to warrior concerns. In the present day, as I have said,
ceremonial dancing continues to be primarily for men, even
though women have been allowed into the dance arena in recent years.

The dance movements and steps are learned by watching
the older members of the tribe dancing and by listening to the
drumbeats. Often very young boys are introduced to the dance
and then become a part of the men's dancing circle by literally
following in their fathers' footsteps. All of the oral sources say
that they were not taught the dance in any formal way, but

"knew" intuitively what to do from the drumbeats, and that the "feeling" they got from the drumbeats is what they interpreted in their movements.

There is not only a flow of music within a set, but also a smooth flow of dance and movement as the dancers circle the drum and go on and off the dance floor. Each afternoon and evening dance opens with a song to which no one dances. When the drumbeats and singers' voices begin on the second song, the dancers rise from their benches, adjust the long otter trailers of their ceremonial dress, and move out to dance around the drum in a counterclockwise circle as the Whipmen circle in a clockwise direction until the benches have been checked for reluctant dancers. "A contemporary free dance" is the best expression to describe what happens in the Osage I'n-Lon-Schka dancing. Each dancer chooses a basic step such as the toe-heel (discussed later in this chapter) and then moves his head, arms, shoulders, and torso in his own individual response to the songs, drumbeats, and tempos, reflecting in his body movements his family clan (gens), the words of the song, or his own feelings. Archie Mason describes the best dancers as those whose roaches, bells, and sashes are dancing with them.[6]

The Osages were divided into gentes in their early history before the arrival of Europeans. Each gens chose as a life symbol a bird, animal, plant, or tree that symbolized strength, beauty, grace, and courage to them. Among these life symbols were the hawk, which symbolized the courage of the warrior; the deer, which gave to the warriors its fleetness; and the elk, which symbolized the entire earth and was helpful in making it into a suitable abode.[7] In earlier I'n-Lon-Schkas there was a full representation of the different family clans present. In the 1970s and 1980s many of the clans are no longer represented; however, some of the clans may still be identified by the dancers' imitating the movements of the animals such as the eagle, buffalo, pheasant, and bear, which are the life symbols of the family clans. Although each man is free to move in response to the music as he chooses, many of the dancers continue to do the same idiosyncratic movements each year. For example, one dancer each year has a nodding-head motion that resembles that of a bird; another moves with his arms and torso giving the effect of a large animal such as a bear; another moves his arms in the gliding movements of a large bird. The dancers maintain and are known by their individual movements each year.

The most common position of the men in the I'n-Lon-Schka is a straight, relaxed, dignified, upright posture with knees slightly bent and arms and hands hanging naturally at the sides (Fig. 17). Often during the chorus of a song when the words of a song are usually sung, changes in body positions and movements occur. It is at this point that some of the dancers appear to be tracking or scouting in a semicrouching position with forearm over forehead in a searching or looking position (Fig. 18). This position is referred to by the Indians as "going down," and the body is brought down from the upright position into a semicrouch or crouch while the basic step is maintained. There is more movement in and out among the dancers at this time; some dancers circling in small, tight circles and others dancing around their coup sticks, which are pointed toward and sometimes touching the ground. At points in the dance some of the dancers face in to the drum, dancing in place for a short period of time. At no time in any dance is the whole assembly of dancers doing exactly the same thing at the same time, aside from moving in the counterclockwise direction around the drum. Each dancer's basic step, body positions, and movements reflect his individuality and response to the music, but never do any of the dancers lose the characteristic quiet dignity.

On the outer edges of the men's dance circle, the women circle quietly with their sedate and dignified dance step, which is slower than that of the men. Their basic step is a step-bend, step-bend with a flat-foot step followed by a bend of the knee of the same leg, giving a bobbing effect. Throughout the dances this step never varies, and the women's body positions remain upright with arms at the sides or folded holding their dance shawls. Also on the outer edges of the men's dance circle are a few fancy dancers whose exhibitionist dancing style is restricted to this area of the dance arena. Like the women, the fancy dancers are not a real part of the I'n-Lon-Schka dance, but they are allowed to participate on the fringes of the dance circle. Unlike the women, the fancy dancers are met by the Whipmen and escorted to benches inside the dance arena with the men

Fig. 17. A drawing by Chris Musgrave of the typical
upright position used by the men dancers in the I'n-Lon-Schka.
A feather fan and coup stick are commonly carried.

Fig. 18. A drawing by Chris Musgrave of the
"going-down" position. The body is brought from the upright
position into a semi-crouch or crouch. Characteristic of the
Indian style is the straight back. Head and back are kept in a
straight line and shoulders are not allowed to slump.

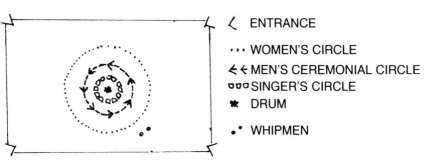

Fig. 19. A diagram of the positions of the
Dancers in the I'n-Lon-Schka dances.

ceremonial dancers. The Whipmen, however, are responsible for seeing that neither the women nor the fancy dancers disturb or crowd the circle of men doing the ceremonial dancing around the drum.

In all Indian dancing there is a certain similarity of movement that identifies it as Indian and that can be called a basic Indian style. Several fundamental steps such as the toe-heel, heel-toe, flat-foot, and flat-heel are the basic steps. Each of these may be done with a double foot action in which both feet participate in each step.[8] These steps are all characteristic of the free dance in which each individual is permitted to dance in the way he chooses.

In the I'n-Lon-Schka dances the most common step is the basic toe-heel step with its variations. The two movements from the toe to the heel on one foot are done to each drumbeat before going on to the same step on the second foot. The reference to the toe here does not actually mean the toe, but the ball of the foot. The knees are kept slightly bent, and pressure is placed on the heel, giving the second beat the accent. This is especially noticeable in the sound of the knee bells, which reflect the second-beat accent in their ching-CHING, ching-CHING. Some dancers give a slight forward thrust on the heel in this step, while others crisscross their feet, adding variety and color to the toe-heel step.

In crisscrossing the toe-heel step, the knees are bent even more to allow for the crossing of feet. Although the toe-heel step is a very simple-looking step, it requires both skill and stamina to do it for an entire afternoon or evening of dancing. The very good dancers demonstrate both agility and control as they use this basic toe-heel step, giving the appearance of barely touching the ground.

Figs. 20 and 21 show the correct position in a toe-heel step and the diagram of a crisscross toe-heel step.

In the heel-toe step the heel touches the ground first before rolling to the ball of the same foot. The step is then repeated on the second foot. I have seen a quick move back to the heel of this same step resulting in a rocking motion from the heel to the ball of the foot and back to the heel. In the flat-heel step, the foot is brought down flat, and the heel is then lifted and lowered on the same beat before repeating the step in the second foot.[9] In this step the feet remain closer to the ground than

Fig. 20. The correct toe-heel position.
(From Bernard S. Mason, *Dances and Stories of the American Indian*)

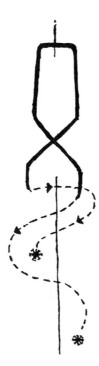

Fig. 21. The crossed toe-heel step diagram.
(From Bernard S. Mason, *Dances and Stories of the American Indian*)

in the toe-heel step. In the flat-foot step, a step is taken on the left foot flat, followed by a skip on the left foot flat before repeating the step on the right foot. In all of these basic steps the knees are kept slightly bent and the steps are not large, keeping the feet always under the body.

Another type of step that is important in the I'n-Lon-Schka is that of the trot or flat-foot trot, which is used during the trot songs in the Saturday night dances. This step is a trot on the left foot flat followed by a trot on the right foot flat, giving the effect of easy running steps, shorter though than in ordinary walking. The step is done very lightly, with the body and knees relaxed. The knees are usually brought up higher than in the toe-heel

Fig. 22. A drawing by Chris Musgrave of the typical arm positions in I'n-Lon-Schka dancing. *Top:* The elbows show rounder angles. *Bottom:* The elbows show sharper angles as the arms are lifted high across the chest.

step. The lack of accent on the second beat is noticeable in the dancers' knee bells, which ring evenly—ching-ching, ching-ching.[10]

There are possible variations of all of the basic steps in which a jump has been added. For example, many of the Tail Dancers do a double toe-heel in which they jump on both toes, heels raised, then drop the left heel, raising the right foot forward before jumping on both toes and repeating the step with the right heel lowered.[11] Many other possibilities also may be used, but these are among some of the commonly used steps in the I'n-Lon-Schka dances. Each man chooses his favorite basic step and keeps it throughout the dances with some variations and embellishments.

The most common position for the hands and arms is hanging naturally at the sides fully relaxed. Sometimes the hands are placed on the hips with the knuckles resting against the back and the fingers pointed downward. Sometimes the arms are brought together in positions across the chest, as in Fig. 22. The upright body position is the most common, but it is a relaxed upright position and not a tense one. This is changed for the "going-down" position in the choruses of some of the songs. The semicrouch is the most difficult to hold, as the back must be kept straight if it is done in the correct Indian style. Both the crouch and semicrouch positions are used when a close-to-the-ground effect is desired by the dancer.

The finales of each dance are usually individualized by the dancers. As the ending approaches, the dancer prepares his finish, often dropping into a crouch and rising on the last beat, kicking the right leg across in front of his left knee on the final beat and holding it there for a moment after the drumming has stopped. Each man responds to the song being sung in his own way, interpreting the meaning of the song for him in his dance movements and steps. As the final drumbeats sound at the end of an evening, each dancer leaves having contributed by his dancing to an interpretation of the meaning of the I'n-Lon-Schka for himself and for his tribe. After the evening dance, the dancers return to their camps or homes, and respect for the drum is reflected in their quiet behavior and departure.

6. The Osage Traditional Dress

It is customary that the dancers wear the Osage traditional ceremonial dress in the I'n-Lon-Schka. A dancer without such a costume will not be permitted into the dance arena, with one exception, as we shall see. This rule is in contrast to the powwow dances, in which dancers appear in a variety of costumes ranging from the elaborate feather-bustled fancy-dance costume to the traditional straight-dance costume to contemporary street attire. The only time in which dancers may dance during the I'n-Lon-Schka without the traditional Osage dress is on the fourth day of the dances, during the family song and give-away day.

Some thirty separate pieces constitute the Osage traditional dress. The cost per costume in the 1970s and 1980s averaged from $1,500 to $3,000 depending on the amount of beadwork, finger weaving, ribbon work, and jewelry used in the decorations. Thirty to forty-five minutes must be allowed for dressing before the dance.

It is customary that no Osage traditional dress is handed down. Each dancer has his own costume custom-made. The revival of interest by the young dancers in recent decades has helped to stimulate and revive the Osage arts of ribbon work and finger weaving essential to the tribal traditional dress. In the late 1960s these were almost lost arts, as very few Osages remained who knew them. Maudie Cheshewalla, curator of the Osage Tribal Museum in Pawhuska, Oklahoma, encouraged the revival of ribbon work and finger weaving in the early 1970s by offering classes at the museum through the Emergency Employment Act.[1] She has taught several hundred women the art of finger weaving, and by the late 1980s women in Pawhuska, Grayhorse, Hominy, and other nearby towns had become well known for their talents in creating the Osage traditional dress for both family members and others.

Work on individual pieces of dress often begins a year before the dance, with the women sewing and weaving all year in preparation for the next I'n-Lon-Schka. These seamstresses take great pride in seeing their finger-woven belts, beaded moccasins, beaded belts, and ribbon work on dance shawls, leggings, and skirts worn by the dancers in each village at the I'n-Lon-Schka. According to Maudie Cheshewalla, "Our tribal council is very aware of the arts now which can be lost, and more effort is made to be sure this doesn't happen. I think, too, more young people are interested in tribal customs and maintaining them than twenty-five years ago."[2]

Although it is customary that no Osage traditional dress is handed down intact, certain elements of decoration, such as silver buckles, pins, bracelets, beaded medallions, and some finger weaving, may be reused. Archie Mason described how he received his roach from Chief Bacon Rind, his knee bells from Andrew Big Horse, a neckerchief holder from his uncle, a large silver medallion from his grandfather, who had received it from Franklin Pierce, and some beautiful beaded medallions from his father.[3]

It is typical of the Osages to mix the colors of the different pieces of their dress to create a vivid effect from many different and contrasting hues. The most commonly used material in the basic pieces of the traditional dress is wool broadcloth with rainbow selvage. The visual effect of the colors and designs of the ribbon work, beadwork, and finger weaving used to decorate this material reflects both family and individual experiences. Just as the dance steps and movements in the I'n-Lon-Schka dances reflect the dancer, the selection of color combinations, decorations, and ornaments reflects the personality and individuality of the wearer of the Osage traditional dress, as in the case when one dancer added Vietnam ribbons and medals to his dress.

Typical examples of the Osage men's traditional dress are seen in Fig. 23. The separate pieces of Osage traditional dress for men, and the materials from which they are made, are as follows:

Leggings of wool broadcloth or buckskin
Breechcloth or g-string of wool broadcloth and cotton or buckskin
Trailer of otter fur

Fig. 23. Examples of Osage men's traditional dress
are shown by Tim and Russ Tallchief.

Drag of wool broadcloth
Shirt of silk
Large scarf of silk
Scarf or handkerchief holder of metal or elk horn
Head roach made from a deer tail dyed red
Roach spreader of metal or elk horn
Eagle feather and attachments to be placed in the roach
Scalp feather—an eagle feather or feather of another large bird
Belt of beaded or nail-studded leather
Moccasins of buckskin
Garters of wool with finger weaving or beaded
Sash of wool with finger weaving
Two strings of large beads
Knee bells of metal on a leather band
Small ribbons and scarves of silk
Coup stick of wood
Fan of eagle feathers or feathers of a large bird
Arm bands of silver or animal horn
Bracelets of silver with turquoise
Blanket of wool broadcloth
Sweat band of cotton

At Grayhorse in June, 1987, the young men prepared for the Friday evening dances as the first bells began to ring. Every piece of their traditional dress was carefully unpacked and laid out on tabletops before they began to dress. Taking care to see that each piece was secured and fastened, they dressed from the feet up to the very top.

In dressing and assembling the costume, the dancer begins with the breechcloth, which is anchored around the waist by a leather belt. The leggings are pinned to the breechcloth and are further supported by woven garters at the knees, over which the knee bells on a leather band are placed. If buckskin leggings are worn, the garters are not necessary, as the buckskin material stays in place better than the wool. An additional sash is tied around the top of the breechcloth. In earlier times a wide, finger-woven cummerbund was used instead of the sash, with the cummerbund ends trailing down the back of the costume from under the shirt. The drag is attached to the breechcloth in back and drags the ground. The bright, multicolored silk shirt is worn over the top of the breechcloth, with a wide beaded and nail-studded leather belt over the shirt at the waist (Fig. 23). At the back, hanging from the neck to the feet, is the otter trailer decorated according to each individual's taste. In 1976, Archie Mason redesigned the decorations of the otter trailer he was to wear in the I'n-Lon-Schka, using beautiful beaded medallions made by and given to him by his father. Many of the otter decorations reflect the family symbols or the life of the individual wearing the otter.

The head roach in recent decades (described in chapter 3) is tied on the head by rawhide thongs under the chin and at the back of the head. The band around the forehead serves both as a sweatband and as a help in holding the roach thongs in place. The large silk scarf is worn around the neck loosely, held in place by the scarf holder. The two strings of large beads are crisscrossed both in front and in back, with the ends fastened under the large belt at the waist (Fig. 23). The scalp feathers are worn dangling from the side of the head, fastened in the hair. The arm bands of silver or horn, with ribbons often tied to them, are worn over the sleeve of the shirt high on the forearm. Other ornaments are bracelets worn at the wrists, silver pins decorating the front of the shift, and bead chokers worn at the neck. Blankets are often worn over the traditional dress into the dance arena. They are then carefully folded and placed on the bench where the dancer will sit, serving as a cushion as well as reserving a dancer's place on the bench.

Several colors—yellow, white, black, blue, and red—were used as face paint in the early I'n-Lon-Schkas. The significance of these colors has been lost. In modern times the Osages use very little face paint in the I'n-Lon-Schka. Usually only a streak of red one finger wide is used from the edge of the eye to the earlobe, a pinch of red is placed on each earlobe, and an outline of red is used around the lips. Red is the most important tribal color to the Osages and symbolizes earth, sun, peace, and friendship.

When women participate in the I'n-Lon-Schka, their relative unimportance is emphasized by the fact that they may do so without the Osage women's traditional dress. Although many women do wear the full traditional dress, they may dance with only a dance shawl over their contemporary street attire if they so choose. However, only those women in the

Osage traditional dress may be seated inside the dance arena on the benches when space is available.

The separate pieces in the Osage traditional dress for women are as follows:

Leggings of wool broadcloth or buckskin
Skirt of wool broadcloth
Garters of wool finger weaving
Wide cummerbund sash or belt of wool finger weaving
Moccasins of buckskin
Blouse of silk
Ribbons, both wide and narrow, of silk
Silver pins
Multistrand glass beads
Silver earrings
Silver arm band
Silver bracelets
Blanket or dance shawl of wool broadcloth or silk with a wide
    fringe

Georgeann Robinson, an authority on as well as creator of many of the custom-made Osage traditional dresses for both men and women in the 1970s, described the assembling of the Osage women's traditional dress as well as the particular dress, shown in Fig. 24, that she created.[4] The women's wool broadcloth leggings are anchored with yarn garters at the knee and then folded around the ankles and tucked into the moccasins in order to make them fit smoothly and stay in place. The ribbon work is on the sides of the leggings. The Osage skirt, made from a large folded piece of wool broadcloth, gives a two-tiered effect with the rainbow selvage of the material (Fig. 26). The wool broadcloth of the skirt is folded and then wrapped around the waist, with a piece of braided string under the fold tied around the waist to hold it in place. The ribbon work decoration usually appears on the side of the wraparound skirt, but in the older-style skirt, shown in Fig. 24, the ribbon work also covers the lower half of the skirt as well. This older skirt was adapted by Mrs. Robinson from one made in the early 1900s belonging to Eva Little Star. The horse in the design is thought to have had special significance for the Little Star family. The small bells on the hem of this skirt were a feature of Osage

Fig. 24. Georgeann Robinson models an Osage traditional dress for women which she adapted from an older dress belonging to Eva Little Star and worn in the early 1900s. Over her arm she is carrying a traditional navy broadcloth blanket trimmed with glass bead decorations.

skirts in the 1920s. The wool broadcloth with rainbow selvage is typical of that used in the Osage traditional dress now and in the past. This material comes only in navy blue and red with the colorful selvage (see Fig. 26).

A wide cummerbund sash of finger weaving is placed over the top of the skirt, with the ends of the cummerbund hanging down the back of the skirt. A silk blouse is placed over the skirt and covers the top of the cummerbund, leaving only the ends visible down the back. The black blouse shown in Fig. 24 is not the usual color chosen for the I'n-Lon-Schka dress unless the wearer is in mourning. Attached at the neck of the blouse in back are the wide, multicolored striped silk ribbons. Beautiful big silver pins, multiple strands of glass beads, beaded or tortoise hairpulls, silver earrings, and silver bracelets are typical of the jewelry worn with the Osage traditional women's dress. A favorite silver earring often worn by Osage women is a silver circle with three small silver teardrops at the bottom of the circle. The hair worn loose signifies mourning, but also is worn in this fashion by older women. Most girls wear one braid down the back. The feather fan is carried in the dance as a "hot fan"—to be used for cooling.

The navy broadcloth blanket with beading and ribbon work on the edge is typical of the blankets worn by Osage women over their traditional dress in the dance. In Fig. 24 Georgeann Robinson is carrying such a blanket over her arm. Colorful striped blankets are also used in the I'n-Lon-Schka dance by the women, and the stripes in such a blanket must be worn vertically to be correct in the Osage style. The Osage moccasins are decorated with a single row of beads and are low-cut with two small buckskin tabs at the heel (Fig. 25). When the high moccasin is worn, it replaces the leggings, but the broadcloth leggings and the low-cut moccasins are most commonly worn by the Osages.[5]

One of the most interesting of the Osage women's costumes is the Osage bridal dress used on special occasions and for special ceremonies within the I'n-Lon-Schka as well as for Osage weddings (Fig. 26). The Osage bridal coat is basically a Revolutionary War officer's dress coat, with gold epaulets and brass buttons, and decorated with Osage ribbon work, finger weaving, and beadwork plus the traditional silver medallions

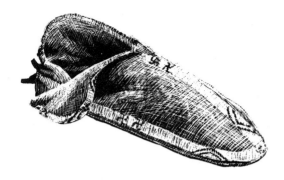

Fig. 25. A drawing by Tom Russell of the typical low-cut
moccasion used in the Osage traditional dress.

and buckles that were once used for trading. The headdress is
similar to a stovepipe hat covered with feathers and ribbons.[6]

According to one historian, this costume came to the
Osages about 1803 after the Louisiana Purchase and after President Thomas Jefferson had invited the leading Osage men to
come to Washington, D.C. Jefferson had hoped to convince the
Osages of the power of the new United States of America as
well as to seek their friendship because of their reputation as
great warriors. He gave them presents of silver medals and dress
tunics worn by the U.S. officers of the period. When the Osage
men returned to the tribe, they gave the tunics to the Osage
brides for their wedding ceremonies.[7] These wedding coats are
greatly prized heirlooms in Osage families and are carefully
handed down, contrary to the custom of not handing down
other kinds of Osage traditional dress. The wedding coats are
worn with the traditional wrap-around blanket skirt, leggings,
and beaded moccasins. Around the waist of the wedding coat is
worn a sash of finger weaving. Carried over the arm is a colorful fringed dance shawl decorated with ribbon work. This
shawl is a prized gift in some Osage ceremonies.[8]

There was a great deal of history, symbolism, and tribal
meaning in the various motifs, colors, and pieces of the nineteenth-century Osage traditional dress. Although much of this
symbolism has been lost in the 1970s and 1980s, with motifs
and colors being used primarily for decorative purposes, tribal

Fig. 26. An Osage bridal dress worn by one of the "brides,"
Vivian Hickey Frick, in the acceptance-of-the-drum ceremony
in the 1975 Grayhorse I'n-Lon-Schka. Note the two-tiered effect
created by the rainbow selvage on the wool broadcloth
of the skirt.

meaning is still attached to some colors, designs, and pieces of this dress. The eagle feather remains as a symbol of dignity and respect and is used to signify a boy's introduction to the dance. The two buckskin tabs or trailers at the heel of the low-cut Osage moccasins were originally intended to help in concealing a person's tracks (Fig. 25). Feather fans are used not only for the practical purpose of cooling a person in hot weather but also in fanning away evil spirits. The red feather worn on the back of an otter trailer signifies a past injury in battle. The Dance Chairman wears a red feather in his roach, signifying rank. A feather in the hair generally signifies that the person is from a prominent chief's family. A red and blue blanket is worn only by the eldest son, with the red always worn on the left. A solid blue blanket is worn by younger sons. The beaver pillbox headdress has to be earned and indicates that the wearer is a warrior who has performed in an outstanding fashion or is heir to a chief. The coup sticks in earlier times were carried only by those men who had counted coup and distinguished themselves as warriors, but now almost all of the dancers carry coup sticks, and their original significance has been lost.

In ribbon work, the light colors represent the moon, the sun, the sky, and sunlight; red represents earth and life; and the dark blues and black represent day and night. The favorite Osage motif of the diamond symbolizes a man's body; triangles represent tepees; and the arrow signifies protection.[9] Many Osage family clans continue to wear clan symbols on their traditional dress. For example, those dancers belonging to the bear clan would wear paw prints on their costume, and those belonging to the sky clan would wear metal on their costume, especially on the otter trailer. Often the three villages use a particular motif in both finger weaving and ribbon work. Grayhorse uses the spider, Pawhuska uses the arrow, and Hominy uses the chevron to symbolize their respective villages.[10]

Originally the Osages' clothes were made from the skin of deer, wapiti, and buffalo, while claws and bones were used in their jewelry. Even today, synthetic materials are avoided, and only natural materials such as shell, buffalo horn, bear teeth, bones, silver, and turquoise are used in jewelry. There is continuing debate and puzzlement over whether some designs and craft practices originated in Europe or among the Osages. Many

European materials were supplied as gifts to win Indian friendships and alliances in the late seventeenth and early eighteenth centuries when the Indians outnumbered Europeans in America. Silver brooches, hair plates, earrings, and cloth materials were typical gifts. Some ornaments were later copied by Indians and then gradually were freely adapted in design and shape to serve particular Indian needs and tastes. The heavy wool trade cloth in red and dark blue—called stroud cloth— and trade beads of rose quartz from China and Venice were common items used by later eighteenth-century traders in buying pelts and belts from the Indians. There is little doubt that the introduction of new materials into their culture and the adaptation of European patterns and designs into their crafts influenced the development of American Indian art.[11]

The intertribal trading of craft styles in and near Oklahoma created a regional Oklahoma Indian style in which Osage practice is only slightly different from that of neighboring tribes. But there are some Osage crafts of special distinction, especially ribbon work and finger weaving. Ribbon work, as done by the Osages, is a type of ribbon mosaic of a variety of colors appliquéd to wool broadcloth. The ribbon is torn, never cut, into long strips and then cut into the specific designs, with one color basted on top of another. Ribbon work is usually done by hand and can be sewn in three different ways: the modern-day fancy stitch, the traditional straight stitch, and the blind stitch. Any number of color combinations may be used, but the traditional scheme is for the light colors to be in the center and the darker colors on the outside. It is not known whether the Osages knew of this ribbon appliqué decoration before the European traders, but they probably did not.[12]

Gregg F. Stock, director of the Kansas City Museum, said that the technique of ribbon work dates from the late eighteenth century, when French nuns first introduced ribbon appliqué work to the southern Great Lakes tribes. The technique gradually diffused to the Prairie Indians, including the Osages, during the nineteenth century. It was also during this same period that buffalo hide for blanket making was replaced by wool materials such as stroud cloth.[13]

Although many tribes do ribbon work, it is a special favorite of the Osages, with certain designs being their own and others borrowed and traded from other tribes. The diamond design, the extended diamond, the prong, and the arrow are all favorite designs in Osage ribbon work, with the prong design being one of the very old Osage designs. The extended diamond, prong, and diamond are seen in Figs. 27, 28, 29, and 30. The Osages use geometric designs more often than the curved designs of the Woodlands Indians. Horses and hands are also common Osage designs on blankets and dresses decorated with ribbon work. Note the horse in Figs. 24 and 27 and the hand in Fig. 29, both of which came from a friendship blanket. Ordinarily ribbon-work patterns and designs are smaller on the traditional dress than on Osage blankets. For example, the designs in Figs. 27 and 28 are typically used by the Osages on blankets, while the examples in Figs. 29 and 30 are characteristic of the small patterns found on traditional dress decorations.[14]

According to Maudie Cheshewalla, finger weaving is one of the most religious types of art done by the Osages, because the finger-woven articles are only worn at tribal dance time. Among these finger-woven articles are belts, garters, sacred sashes, and the bags used to carry religious articles. Finger

Fig. 27. Osage ribbon-work designs with the horse, extended diamond, arrows, and small diamond. The horse figure is red on a purple field with a white outline. Below the horse the white area is white, followed by green. The bottom band is red (matching the horse) against yellow.

Fig. 28. Osage ribbon work with the extended diamond and the prong. The extended diamond and prong design is yellow against purple at the top and red on the bottom.

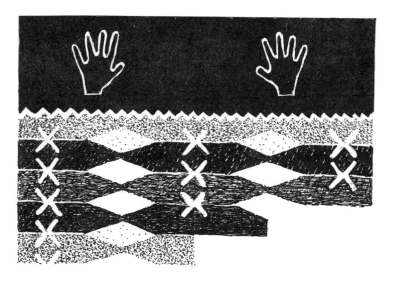

Fig. 29. Osage ribbon-work designs of the small diamonds and the hands. The hand design is red with yellow outline against black. Next is yellow rickrack followed by the background bands in silver, red, green, and purple with the first row of diamond and X shapes in yellow, the second and third rows of diamond and X shapes in white, and the fourth row of diamond and X shapes in yellow.

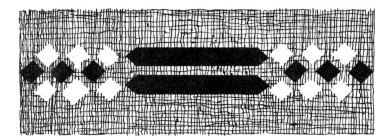

Fig. 30. Osage ribbon-work designs with small diamonds,
typical of the smaller patterns used on the traditional dress.
The background is turquoise with all black shapes
purple and the remaining diamond shapes white.

weaving, sometimes known as Osage braid because of the
tribe's extensive use of this craft, is a very old method of thread
interlacing in which the fingers pick up the vertical warp threads
through which the horizontal weft is passed. The weaving is
worked from the center to the outside edges and is a very tight
weaving, giving much the same effect as tapestry weaving.
Wool yarn is most commonly used now, but both buffalo hair
and human hair were used in the earlier times before wool
yarn. In earlier times the women sat on the ends of the strands
of wool yarn. Today they tie the yarn strands to a solid support
such as the back of a chair or a stand (Fig. 31). With the development of finger weaving it became possible to weave many new
geometric designs for use in ceremonial sashes, garters, and
headbands. According to Maudie Cheshewalla, the Osages are
about the only ones who weave with so many different patterns. They are also the only ones who use beads in their
weaving.[15]

The debate whether the finger weaving method was aboriginal or introduced, and whether the designs were influenced
by European embroidery taught in mission schools or were
original designs among the Osages, will probably never be
completely resolved. However, the French probably are the
sources of such favorite Osage designs as the chevron, the
double chevron, and the fleur-de-lis. Other favorite designs,
such as the spider, the arrow, the diamond, and the double diamond,[16] are probably Osage in origin. The Osage tribe alone

uses the double diamond in its finger weaving. These last designs appeared as motifs on Osage tents, costumes, and artifacts
from before the Europeans' arrival. For example, the spider motif
is known to have been a life symbol of one of the old gentes. The
spider was chosen because, like the Osage, "he builds his home
where he is and all things come to him."[17] The spider motif
appears on the entrance floor of the Osage Tribal Museum
in Pawhuska, Oklahoma. It is believed that the Osage simply
transferred these older motifs to the new materials and crafts,
such as ribbon work, which came with the Europeans (Figs. 31,
32, and 33).

Even after her many years of practice, Maudie Cheshewalla
could only work some six hours a day in finger weaving, com-
pleting about one inch per hour. A woman's sash took her about
two months to complete. Considered an authority in finger
weaving, she had the ability to take an old pattern—even one a

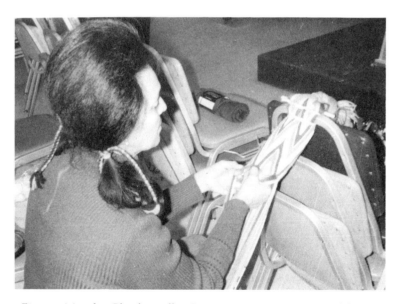

Fig. 31. Maudie Cheshewalla, Osage Museum curator and finger
weaving instructor, finger weaving with yarn strands tied to the
back of a chair. The design is the double chevron, and
the weaving will be a wide ceremonial sash.

hundred years old—and figure it out. Because of this ability she was often called on by museums to repair or copy some of their unusual and important pieces of finger weaving.[18]

Osage beadwork, although used a great deal in Osage traditional dress, is similar in design to that of other tribes and not so distinctly an Osage craft as are finger weaving and ribbon work. Beads were introduced among the Plains tribes in the early part of the nineteenth century, and beadwork gradually replaced the older traditions of quillwork and embroidery. The early beads were fairly large, of a type known as pony beads, and were mostly white, black, and blue. Consequently, the designs of the Plains Indian beadwork are in bold designs of either blue and white or black and white. These colors were the cheapest to produce and gave the greatest margin of profit to traders. Today the red and yellow beads still cost more to produce. The smaller glass beads known as seed beads were used on the western Plains as early as 1830. By that time the western Plains Indians were in a position to obtain any of the trade items commonly used in trading with the eastern Indians.[19] The large tubular beads used on many of the Indian costumes today are called hairbone beads. Beadwork appears on

Fig. 32. A drawing of the double-chevron finger-weaving design—a favorite Osage design. The solid black areas are red, the white areas are white with the mottled black areas alternating blue and pink.

Fig. 33. The double-diamond finger-weaving design is the pattern done only by the Osage tribe. The solid black areas are red, with the striped areas dark blue and the white areas white.

the Osage traditional dress especially in the large belt worn over the silk shirt in the men's dress and on the medallions decorating the otter trailer.

These craft traditions were nearly lost, and it is worth noting how they were saved. In the 1930s under President Franklin Roosevelt's Works Progress Administration (WPA), Federal Art Project No. 1 sponsored a program for the preservation of Native American culture. The program brought to public attention for the first time the richness of this heritage and ultimately brought into being the Osage Tribal Museum in Pawhuska, which is not only a repository for Osage artifacts but also a center for the preservation and stimulation of such uniquely Osage crafts as finger weaving and ribbon work.[20]

The history of this museum dates to 1934, when John Joseph Mathews became interested in the conservation of Osage culture through the WPA-sponsored programs of culture preservation. He was elected an Osage council member in 1934 and formed a committee with George Labadie, an Osage tribal councilman and lawyer, and Petseemoah. Mathews went to Harold Ickes, then secretary of the interior, and Holger Cahill, then director of the Federal Art Project No. 1, with the idea of building an Osage tribal museum on the agency grounds where an old chapel building stood. Working through Ickes and John Collier, who was commissioner of Indian affairs under Roosevelt, Mathews was able to convince Cahill to give government funds to the museum project. The old chapel was torn down, and the new museum began, with the opening on May 8, 1938. There were two celebrations, one for the city and one for the tribe. Mathews continued to take an active interest in the Osage Tribal Museum and did the preliminary work on a proposal for federal funds for the museum as late as the 1970s.[21]

Included in the museum today is a gallery of paintings of the great Osage leaders from the 1930s to the present times as well as a fine collection of photographs of important occasions in twentieth-century Osage history. The 1930s paintings were done by artists sponsored under Federal Arts Project No. 1, but are not the work of Osages. These oil paintings were made possible through a second grant that Mathews put together to finance oil portraits of elderly Osage full-bloods. Most of the portraits were painted by Todros Geller, a Russian-born Chicago artist who was introduced to his subjects by Mathews, who persuaded these elderly Osages to sit for the preliminary sketches.[22]

Also on display in another collection are Osage artifacts from earlier times, such as old weapons, ritual pouches, cradle carriers, and Osage traditional dress. This museum is the home of an Osage oral history project. Vital to the preservation of Osage crafts are the classes taught at the museum in the 1970s and 1980s in ribbon work, finger weaving, beadwork and moccasin making. Classes in the Osage language, history, and culture are also a part of the museum's offerings.

7. New Ways for Old Traditions

One of the more visible changes in the I'n-Lon-Schka since its beginning is the admittance of women dancers into the dance arena after the late 1940s. Historian Terry Wilson suggests that this could be part of the new political power of Osage women, which in itself was an expression of the raising of their social and economic status.[1] Before the forties women were not allowed within the dance arena, as the I'n-Lon-Schka was a warrior society's ceremony. In those earlier days, a woman wanting to dance had to stand in her place outside the dance arena and move to the rhythm of the drum. This is still done today by many of the older women, who simply stand during the song and dance in place to the drumbeat. Even now they must remain on the outside edge of the dance circle and must not intrude upon or interfere with the men's dancing in the circle around the drum.

There is no ceremony for a girl's or woman's introduction to the dance comparable to a boy's. Most of the women are seated outside the dance arena and are not greeted by the Whipmen as the men dancers are. The women simply enter the dance arena quietly after the men have begun to dance. Some women wear the traditional women's dress, but, as has been noted, it is not required for them as it is for the men. At one time, because of damage caused to the dance floor by the stiletto heels of the 1940s and 1950s, women were not allowed into the dance arena unless they wore moccasins. Now there is greater leniency; both moccasins and current styles of shoes are worn by the women dancing in today's I'n-Lon-Schkas. But women dancers are not an essential part of the ceremonies and remain largely incidental to them.

One very important change in the I'n-Lon-Schka traditions that has affected many different aspects of more recent dances is the increase in numbers of dancers since the early days. Before World War II only the eldest sons and members of the three Osage dance organizations were admitted to the dance floor, with invitations sent to a few other tribes on a limited basis. This kept the number of dancers at about sixty. Against the advance of the elders, the number of dancers taking part in the I'n-Lon-Schka was allowed to increase after World War II. Other Indian tribes, Osages who were not eldest sons, and Osages who were not a part of the three Osage dance organizations but who had been introduced to the dance were allowed to dance in the I'n-Lon-Schka, and women also were allowed into the dance arena on the outside edge if space was available.

On a Saturday night in the 1970s and 1980s the dancers often numbered over three hundred. This growth partly accounts for the expansion of the old brush arbors and roundhouses into the present dance arbors. Although the mechanics of the dance have remained basically the same, a much larger dance committee or organization has developed with the increase in the numbers of dancers (see chapter 3). This larger dance organization is partly a result of economics, as it brings a broader financial base which helps to defray the increased costs of the larger dances. It also is necessary in the proper administration of them.

The understanding and interpretation of the I'n-Lon-Schka has had to be kept and reaffirmed in the present-day dances. The diversity of the groups dancing today accounts for changes in or ignorance of some of the old traditions and rules, since some of the dancers may not be aware of them. The participants are looking for a clear definition of the I'n-Lon-Schka. Because of the oral tradition, there are often different interpretations of the ceremonies, and the I'n-Lon-Schka leaders must resolve these within their dance organizations. The larger the dance organization, the more pressure there is on the Drumkeeper and the Dance Chairman, because more organization members mean more differences of opinion. The Dance Chairman and Drumkeeper must resolve these differences before they get away from the intent of the dances. This is done in committee meetings by consensus.[2]

A large portion of the increase in dancers has been among the young, some hardly more than toddlers. With these younger

I'n-Lon-Schka participants has come an important new element. Women are extremely important as the teachers and trainers of the younger dancers, especially those living away from the three Osage villages, and so their attitudes, ideas, and understandings of the dance have become an important force. The Dance Chairman and Drumkeeper must be clear in their interpretations and definitions of the I'n-Lon-Schka traditions for these women, because the women will be spending far more time in training the younger dancers than will the I'n-Lon-Schka leaders. With the younger generation of dancers have come many more questions about the conduct of the dance. Because many of these younger dancers have not been raised in the traditional Native American way and have grown up in an urban environment rather than a close Osage community such as Grayhorse, it is difficult for them to understand the meaning behind the traditions that earlier I'n-Lon-Schka dancers took for granted.[3]

In the early days of the I'n-Lon-Schka the family units were closer, with most family members living in the same village or area and often whole families participating in their village I'n-Lon-Schka. In the 1950s, when today's I'n-Lon-Schka leaders were growing up in these villages, they were not brought into the dance until they were old enough to know what was happening and how to behave—usually at the age of eight or nine after they had received training in the I'n-Lon-Schka traditions and after their fathers and grandfathers had decided that they were ready. They understood the reasons behind many of the old dance traditions and rules because they grew up with them, while many of the younger dancers of today have not had this background.[4]

Although today's younger dancers have not grown up in a traditional Osage environment, they still have a great respect for the I'n-Lon-Schka and a sincere and vital concern to know its traditions. This adds to the duties and pressures of the Dance Chairmen and Drumkeepers as well as other I'n-Lon-Schka leaders as they interpret the I'n-Lon-Schka traditions for today's participants. Though these younger dancers might not grasp the verbal or written explanations of the I'n-Lon-Schka, they still are able to sense the power, energy, and vitality of the ceremonies and the purpose of support of the I'n-Lon-Schka drum.

More and more of these young dancers who are introduced to the dance remain involved in the dance. The elders of the tribe today are pleased that many young Osages have found in the I'n-Lon-Schka ceremonies a symbol of their Osage identity and that these young dancers have given the ceremonies their enthusiastic support.[5]

Because there are fewer adult dancers in the forty- to fifty-year-old group in proportion to the younger dancers in today's I'n-Lon-Schka, the I'n-Lon-Schka leaders and adults feel a special challenge to reach and train the young dancers correctly. In the early days of the I'n-Lon-Schka, the oral tradition worked smoothly in the close Osage communities of Grayhorse, Pawhuska, and Hominy to communicate the traditions as well as to coordinate and plan the dances. In recent years, when so many family units and members are scattered, and perhaps only one or two in a family are involved in the I'n-Lon-Schka, communication only by oral tradition is more difficult. There was a time when it was not necessary to put the dance traditions into written form, but many of today's leaders feel that it is now necessary, since the nucleus is no longer a small family unit, but the I'n-Lon-Schka drum in Grayhorse, Pawhuska, or Hominy. They feel that the dance and its traditions must be recorded in order to preserve them for the younger members, and that as the leaders, they must rely on the written word as well as the oral tradition. They will be the keepers of the I'n-Lon-Schka history, and much of what is left will be the written word.[6]

Archie Mason, Jr., feels that he and other leaders like him must provide an image for the younger dancers, while also serving as a mirror for them. As he teaches the young dancers the I'n-Lon-Schka traditions, he will make use of both the oral tradition and the written word. His grandfather made the rules, and his father knew the rules, but he and his generation are trying to learn, follow, and interpret those rules as they have been handed down to them from their elders.[7] The oral tradition remains very much in evidence at the dances, as great importance is still placed on the presence of the elders to guide and advise the leaders. Archie Mason, Jr., describes it "as kind of like OJT, on-the-job-training, you know. We're out there in our forties and fifties, and we're novices in this. And our Elders are teach-

ing us, advising us, cautioning us. They caution the youngsters
when they're out of line, doing something improper."[8]

An unusual aspect of the I'n-Lon-Schka in recent years is
that some of the adult men dancers are not veterans of a war,
nor have they served in the military. Originally the I'n-Lon-Schka
was a warrior society, and for many years, as the young dancers
grew into manhood, they joined one of the armed services and
became veterans of a war—World War I, World War II, Korea,
or Vietnam. They earned their coups in the honorable and very
traditional Indian way by proving themselves as men and warriors in battles. Today there are adult dancers who are not veterans of a war yet who are allowed to dance in the I'n-Lon-
Schka alongside that elite group of war veterans. They have
proved themselves as men and warriors through their professional involvements, getting their coups with their pens and
briefcases. The knowledge of the I'n-Lon-Schka is also with
them, although they are not eligible to receive and wear the red
feather because they have not been in battle.[9]

Today's I'n-Lon-Schka depends on a large number of people
who no longer live in their home villages but commute to the
dances. They must shift from their work, professions, and
homes in cities and communities outside of Pawhuska, Hominy,
and Grayhorse back to the old world of the I'n-Lon-Schka in
those three villages. Archie Mason, Jr., describes his life as
"high-flex," as he shifts from being the administrative director
of Indian education in the Tulsa public schools to his position as
Head Tail Dancer for the 1987 Grayhorse I'n-Lon-Schka. Browning Pipestem shifts from being a lawyer in a law firm in
Norman, Oklahoma, to his position as the 1987 Grayhorse
Dance Chairman. Jerry Shaw shifts from his teaching position
at Wichita State University to being the father of 1987
Grayhorse Drumkeeper John Shaw and the head of the host
family for the 1987 Grayhorse I'n-Lon-Schka (see Fig. 9). Ed Red
Eagle, Jr., must shift from being the supply evaluation manager
for Citgo Petroleum in Tulsa, Oklahoma, to his position as a
Whipman for the 1987 Pawhuska I'n-Lon-Schka. A contemporary I'n-Lon-Schka leader who is not a commuter and who is an
exception to those mentioned above is Ed Red Eagle, Sr. (Fig.
34), who continues to live in the Pawhuska Indian village, con-

Fig. 34. Ed Red Eagle, Sr., at the 1987 Pawhuska I'n-Lon-Schka, where he served as Dance Chairman (Head Committeeman).

tinues to serve as the assistant chief of the Osage Nation, and acts as Dance Chairman for the Pawhuska I'n-Lon-Schka. He was the oldest dancer in the 1987 I'n-Lon-Schka.[10]

Preparations and plans for the I'n-Lon-Schka are still made throughout an entire year, as in the past. But the coordination of these plans and preparations between those "within and without" the three Osage I'n-Lon-Schka villages is a real challenge to the commuting dance leaders. They cannot have the same involvement in the I'n-Lon-Schka as did their fathers and grandfathers, who resided in the three Osage villages and lived the I'n-Lon-Schka 365 days a year. In spite of this, they still feel a real responsibility and commitment to preserving and continuing the I'n-Lon-Schka and its traditions.[11] Archie Mason, Jr., said: "We go on and do the best we can. I think that's part of the whole thing . . . finally figuring out what the I'n-Lon-Schka is about, and what it does for you. You take that with you into the world every day, and you get along in a good way because the I'n-Lon-Schka has given that to you."[12]

These commuters—both I'n-Lon-Schka leaders and participants—experience relief in being involved in the I'n-Lon-Schka and get recharged for the whole year through their involvement. They come away from the dance rejuvenated and feeling as if a new year has begun. For them all, it is again a homecoming, providing them with a way of participating in the traditions of their people and satisfying a need for them that is different from their fathers'. Their homecoming prepares them to cope with the frustrations and complexities of the modern world. It also gives them a home base that is particularly important for these twentieth-century nomadic, commuting Osage people of the 1970s and 1980s.[13]

Some additional changes from the old times are seen in the new twentieth-century communication tools that are now in evidence at today's I'n-Lon-Schkas. Aids to the oral communication tradition are seen in the use of tape recorders by the singers. It is very common to see the cassette tape recorders under the singers' chairs or on their laps as they sit around the drum. This is an aid in their study and learning of the I'n-Lon-Schka songs. Also, the Dance Chairmen use the microphone and public address system as they make announcements during the dances; that use probably resulted from the increase in the number of dancers. The Town Crier made the announcements without electronic help in the early I'n-Lon-Schkas.[14] Dancers in the old days were not allowed to smoke until the Dance Chairman smoked. The Dance Chairman passed around a special tobacco mixture of his own to the dancers. Today's dancers bring their own cigarettes and smoke when they wish between the dances.[15] There have been enormous changes in the gifts given during the acceptance-of-the-drum ceremony from the old days, when the new Drumkeeper would give away several horses, two wedding dresses, and a few blankets. In recent years the give-away has greatly increased, as noted in Appendix B. The tremendous expense of the modern-day give-away is an obligation accepted by the Drumkeepers.[16]

In describing both the continuity and change in modern Indian life, Scott Bradshaw, an Osage-Quapaw, noted that summers still are, as they have always been, the special time for both family and tribe. Although he feels that his great-grandfather would not know what was going on if he witnessed a recent dance, he would understand the spirit of the dance, which is still very similar to that of the Indians of old: "The sense of family, the pride of heritage, the seriousness of the occasion, the humor of the moment are the same as they have always been when Indians gather."[17]

8. *Significance of the I'n-Lon-Schka*

The basic belief underlying Indian ceremonies is that the tribe lives in harmony with nature. While this concept has meanings on several levels, the idea of harmony with nature is first of all to be taken literally. The Osage I'n-Lon-Schka occurs during the month of June each year, celebrating the season of new growth—of the rebirth of green grass and corn, so important to the survival of the tribe. The I'n-Lon-Schka is equally important at the symbolic level as a demonstration that the Osages are in harmony and at peace with one another as well as the universe. In this larger sense of living in harmony with nature, the dances allow for a new growth of the spirit, a rebirth of Osage understanding and knowledge of the world with the realization that such understanding has weakened in the course of time. In keeping with the I'n-Lon-Schka spirit, old enmities are put aside, and a new, but very traditional, peace is found with fellow tribal members, members of other tribes, and, now, members of the white society. Reverence and respect for the I'n-Lon-Schka drum, and by extension for all life associated with Osage tradition, is shown at every point in the ceremonies, most obviously in the quiet behavior, open friendliness, and fellowship surrounding the ceremonies.

Wah'Kon-Tah, the Great Spirit of the Osages, is described by Mathews as "that which the children of the earth do not comprehend as they travel the roads of the earth and which becomes clear to them only when they have passed on to the Great Mysteries."[1] Wah'Kon-Tah in the late twentieth century seems to have taken the form of the Christian God, Heavenly Father, Jesus Christ. The appearance of the name Wah'Kon-Tah in many of the songs of the I'n-Lon-Schka is the tribe's way of praising Him and asking for His blessing on the people participating in the I'n-Lon-Schka, the dance itself, and the place.

In histories of the Osages, the tribe has always been noted for its pride in its children, and especially its sons. It is certainly not by chance that an eldest son is chosen for the honored position of Drumkeeper. Not only is choosing an eldest son a means by which a prominent Osage family demonstrates its pride in its son, but also the I'n-Lon-Schka becomes the ceremony of presenting him to the tribe, his introduction, his coming out. Not every Osage son has the opportunity to be the Drumkeeper, but every son may be presented to the tribe through the introduction-to-the-dance ceremony.

Because the Osage tribe is facing many difficult political questions of tribal organization, headrights, voting procedures, allotted and unallotted rights, and blood quantum, the I'n-Lon-Schka in this era is of crucial importance as a means of binding together the members of the tribe who are divided on many issues. The I'n-Lon-Schka music, dance movements, and traditional dress all serve to remove the participants from the white world and its everyday concerns to the world of Indian culture. As Ed Red Eagle said in the 1976 I'n-Lon-Schka in his introductory remarks: "We do not come here dressed like this just for appearance. We have come here in our traditional dress to dance in the way of our people, our ancestors—parents and grandparents—since 1884."[2] Archie Mason, Jr., says: "The I'n-Lon-Schka supports the people in times of joy and tragedy and goes on in spite of them. It passes on traditions and gives them a feeling of belonging and properness from generation to generation. There is a belief in that dance because the I'n-Lon-Schka will go on, and the spirits and memories of those who went before are still there and prepare the people for another world."[3]

The dances, therefore, are not sentimental ritual but an act of cultural self-preservation. Each participant is, for these four days, at one with his Indian heritage and by his participation reclaims those Osages in attendance from their year-long allegiance to white culture. The dances are the means by which Osages preserve their strong identity as Indians while also coexisting successfully in the white world. Living in harmony with nature and human nature has never been easy.

In the I'n-Lon-Schka, music, dance, and costume interact with each other to produce a total effect. The music of the voices and the drum influence the execution of the dance movements and the responses of individual dancers. The variations from fast to slow tempos and the dynamic changes are paralleled in the dancers' movements around the drum. The individual dancers respond to the dramatic changes experienced in the tempos and move from a prayer song to a warrior song. The array of colors in the traditional dresses of the dancers, as well as the mass movements of the dancers on the floor together, produce a stimulating visual effect. There is a tremendous excitement about the I'n-Lon-Schka experience when music, dance, and costume interact with each other not merely as the performance of an art form but also as an interplay of each individual's existence within a generations-old group. It is the nurture and sustenance of the act of renewing a tradition, all the more vital since it survives within a white culture that has been unfriendly to it.

It would be a mistake to think that the experience of the I'n-Lon-Schka is limited to the few days of the performances each June. The actual days of the ceremony are only a part of the experience. The people and districts involved in the dances are involved throughout the entire year so that the I'n-Lon-Schka becomes a way of life. The leaders of the dance organization are aware of how important it is to maintain a closeness among the participants and others in the host villages. There is an involvement of a mystical sort, an anticipation of joining a continuing force and aiding in energizing it. There is no break in the maintenance of the force, since as the ceremonies are concluded for one year, the preparations have already begun for the next year's ceremonies. In spite of weather ranging from blazing hot summer days to tornadic winds, the dancers appear in full traditional dress and dance both afternoon and evening. The modern-day weather forecast has little significance in the concept of nature to the Osage.

In studying the I'n-Lon-Schka, I have not found answers to a number of questions. They constitute a rich field for further research. Those that concern me most, and for which I wish I had even the most tentative answers, are: What is the meaning of the song texts and vocables to the participants? What is the relationship of the I'n-Lon-Schka with the peyote religion? What is the role of women in the I'n-Lon-Schka?

Such surface meanings as can be gained through straightforward translation of song texts are inadequate. There are special symbolic significances, many of which are of a highly personal and individualistic kind. Similarly, what is the nature of the influence of the texts and vocables on dance movements, and is it not likely that clusters and levels of meaning are held by family clans that are not shared with others? Or to what extent do the texts contain words and references whose meanings may have been obscured or lost over the years and decades?

Although the peyote religion and the I'n-Lon-Schka came to the Osages in the 1880s at approximately the same time, according to Ed Red Eagle and Archie Mason, they were separate entities. When the I'n-Lon-Schka and peyote religion first came to the Osages, a man had to choose one or the other and could not be a member of both. Later the rules of the I'n-Lon-Schka were changed to allow a young man who had joined the peyote religion to be able to join the I'n-Lon-Schka also. Ed Red Eagle's grandfather and Chief Bacon Rind both joined the I'n-Lon-Schka and kept only with it. His father "went with the peyote religion," and then later he was allowed to join the I'n-Lon-Schka too. The two ceremonies remained separate even though a person could be a member of both. During this period when a person could belong to both the I'n-Lon-Schka and to the peyote religion, the children were often given their Indian name first in the peyote service and therefore would already have their Indian name as they joined the I'n-Lon-Schka. In recent times there are not as many who are members of the Native American (Peyote) Church and most children come now to the I'n-Lon-Schka without their Indian names. Before they join the I'n-Lon-Schka they must once again have the old name-giving ceremony.[4]

There remains an active Native American Church in a few villages, but Osage membership in this church has declined to only 150 active worshipers, or five fireplaces, according to Leroy Logan.[5] Some Indians, both in earlier times and now, practiced the peyote religion and the Christian faith without apparent conflict. Chief Fred Lookout, for example, received two funeral services—a Catholic mass and a peyote church service.

As already noted in chapter 7, the role of women in the I'n-Lon-Schka has steadily increased in the last half of the twentieth century. The appearance of women within the dance arenas in the 1940s reflected their increased political power. To-day women play an increasing role in the transmission of the I'n-Lon-Schka traditions to their families and are actively involved in the training of the young I'n-Lon-Schka dancers. Women almost always stand up with the young men or boys who are introduced to the dance. They help in the preparation of the traditional dress for each dancer and are continuing the old art forms of finger weaving and ribbon work. In recent years women as well as men are considered elders in the three Osage villages. For example, special credit was given to Mary Lookout Standing Bear during the Pawhuska I'n-Lon-Schka centennial celebration when she was thanked for "always being there when we need her."[6]

Another continuing role of women from times past is in their participation as cooks. Special recognition is always given to the cooks who provide the numerous meals during the four days of the I'n-Lon-Schka in each village. These meals are still an important part of the celebration. Browning Pipestem gave special thanks to the cooks in both the Pawhuska and Hominy 1987 I'n-Lon-Schkas. He thanked them for standing over their hot fires on these 100-degree-plus days, cooking the traditional fried bread, corn soup, and beef soup. The preparation of the food as well as the cooking is all a part of the ceremony.[7]

Further investigation is needed, of course, to compare the Osage patterns and practices with those of other closely related Indian tribal rites, as well as those more remote, in order to as-certain similarities and significant differences in a broader frame of reference. Bearing in mind, however, that the descriptions herein are of a living and constantly evolving art form, it would be foolish to conclude that the final word has been spoken. This chapter, then, might well be considered as one of conclusions in which nothing can be concluded. Whatever future historians may discover or disclose, the preceding pages may with cer-tainty be said to contain a unique record of the status of Osage ceremonials and practices as performed during the 1970s and 1980s. It may also be stated that this study has presented an important episode in the arts, attitudes, and understanding of a still-living tradition of a culture within a culture, a picture within a picture, existing in the vastly expanded panorama of contemporary America.

Appendix A

Grayhorse District 1975–76
I'n-Lon-Schka Organization

Drumkeeper
Curtis Oren Bear (age nine years)

Committeemen
Browning Pipestem (Head or Chairman)
Francis Drexil
Joe Bates, Jr.
Cody Tucker
Girard Fish
Omar Jefferson, Jr.
Teddy Mashburn (son of the Head Cook)
King Bowman (former Drumkeeper)
Lester Williams
Clay Donelson
Raymond Lasley, Jr.
Gil Daniels

Advisors
Anthony Daniels (Head)
Archie Mason, Sr. (former Dance Chairman)
Harold West, Sr.
Pierce St. John, Sr.
John Blackbird

Cooks
Loreen Mashburn (Head)
Mary Williams
Mary Green
Clara Belle Brumley
Frances Rhodes
Maudie Cheshewalla (museum curator and finger weaving expert)
Nora Stuart
Helen Robertson

Water Carriers
Charles Tillman, Jr.
Terril Mixson
John Whitesell, Jr.

Tail Dancers
Archie Mason, Jr. (Head)
Johnathan Goode
Ronnie Goodeagle
Anthony Lookout (son of Morris Lookout, Head Singer)
Arthur Cox
Richard Roberts

Whipmen
Charles Tallchief (replaced by Francis Sweetwater, Jr., because of a
   broken leg)
Jerry Shaw

Drum Warmer
Vernon Butler

Singers (Men)
Morris Lookout (Head)
Harry Buffalohead
Albert Waters
Joe Rush
Jim Clark
Adam Le Clair
Jack Anquoe
Russell Rush
Napoleon Le Clair
Lionel Le Clair

Women Singers
Alice Little Cook
Lucy Crys for Ribs
Bessie Le Clair
Leonra Buffalohead
Georgia Le Clair

Town Crier
Raymond Tyndall

Appendix B

Gifts Presented at the Acceptance-of-the-Drum Ceremony, Grayhorse I'n-Lon-Schka, June, 1975

Mrs. Gertrude Sroufe—Osage dance shawl decorated with Osage ribbon work
King Bowman, former Drumkeeper and grandson of Mrs. Sroufe—wool Indian blanket, Palomino quarterhorse filly
Mrs. Barbara Bowman, mother of King Bowman—Osage wedding dress
Mrs. Gertrude Sroufe—Osage wedding dress
Mrs. Lorena Mashburn—Osage wedding dress
Mrs. Josephine Tillman—Osage wedding dress
Browning Pipestem, new Dance Chairman—Osage robe decorated with Osage ribbon work
Joe Bates, Jr.—Osage robe with Osage ribbon work
Cody Tucker—Indian striped wool blanket
Girard Fish—Indian striped wool blanket
Omar Jefferson, Jr.—Indian striped wool blanket
King Bowman—Indian striped wool blanket
Lester Williams—Indian striped wool blanket
Clay Donelson—Indian striped wool blanket
Raymond Lasley, Jr.—Indian striped wool blanket
Gil Daniels—Indian striped wool blanket
Anthony Daniels—wool blanket with Osage ribbon work
Archie Mason, Sr.—blanket with Osage ribbon work
Harold West—blanket with Osage ribbon work
Pierce St. John—blanket with Osage ribbon work
John Blackbird—blanket with Osage ribbon work
Loreen Mashburn—dance shawl
Mary Williams—dance shawl
Mary Green—dance shawl
Clara Belle Brumley—dance shawl
Frances Rhodes—dance shawl with embroidery (yellow)
Maudie Cheshewalla—dance shawl with embroidery (red)

Helen Tallchief Robertson—dance shawl
Charles Tillman, Jr.—Indian striped wool blanket
Terril Mixson—Indian striped wool blanket
Archie Mason, Jr.—Indian striped wool blanket
Johnathan Goode—Indian striped wool blanket
Ronnie Goodeagle—Indian striped wool blanket
Anthony Lookout—Indian striped wool blanket
Carl Cox—Indian striped wool blanket
Richard Roberts—Indian striped wool blanket
Charles Tallchief—Indian striped wool blanket
Jerry Shaw—Indian striped wool blanket
Vernon Butler—Indian striped wool blanket
Morris Lookout—Indian striped wool blanket
Harry Buffalohead—Indian striped wool blanket

All the other men and women singers, as well as the Town Crier, Raymond Tyndall, received Indian striped wool blankets during this acceptance-of-the-drum ceremony. The investment in the Indian blankets and dance shawls alone is a considerable one, with the blankets costing from $38 to $50 apiece. The shawls and blankets with ribbon work cost between $60 to $80 apiece. The Osage bride dresses cost between $500 to $700. Without question, the obligations of presenting these gifts represents a very large expense to the new Drumkeeper and his family.

Appendix C

Individual and Family Songs at the Grayhorse I'n-Lon-Schka, June 5, 1975

Drumkeeper
Committeemen
Jamison Bear
Henry Tallchief
Wilson Kirk
Victor Akers
Hunk-A-Hoppy
Mike Watson
Joe Mason
Ida Bates Sweetwater
Frank Shaw
Archie Mason
Louis Red Eagle
Francis Pipestem
Hall Goode, Jr.
Lillie Burkhart
Cody Tucker
Johnny Williams
Martha Donelson
Thomas Lane
Alfred McKinley
Pierce St. John
Whipmen
Cooks
Women Singers

Notes

Preface

1. From the certificate of competency which I received from the federal government upon my twenty-first birthday. This document certifies that the person named of Indian extraction is both literate and competent to manage his or her own affairs. Since 1948 this certificate is issued automatically to any Indian of less than one-half Indian blood. Before 1948 proof of competency was necessary before the certificate could be issued. This process is discussed further in chapter 1.

2. Tayrien is Americanized from French Terrien, and Canville from Quenneville.

3. Manuscript paper by Mrs. Virginia Marsh, read by her before the Neosho County Historical Society in October, 1930. Shaw family records in the collection of Mrs. Ben Yassek, Bartlesville, Oklahoma.

4. This historical marker is located in the center of Shaw on U.S. Highway 59.

Introduction

1. Julia M. Buttree, *Rhythm of the Redman*, p. 3.

2. Frances Densmore, *American Indians and Their Music*, p. 59; Bruno Nettl, *An Introduction to Folk Music in the United States*, p. 24.

3. Bernard S. Mason, *Dances and Stories of the American Indian*, p. 4; Arnold Marquis, *A Guide to America's Indians*, p. 67.

4. Densmore, *American Indians*, p. 31.

5. John Collier, *The Indians of the Americas*, p. 366; Morris Lookout interview, August, 1975.

6. Archie Mason, Jr., interview, June, 1987.

7. Charles Hamm, Bruno Nettl and Ronald Byrnside, *Contemporary Music and Music Cultures*, p. 113; Frances Densmore, *Teton Sioux Music*, p. 86; Collier, *Indians of the Americas*, p. 233.

Chapter 1. Cultural and Historical Beginnings

1. John Joseph Mathews, *The Osages: Children of the Middle Waters*, p. 349; David Baird, *The Osage People: Centennial Issue, 1872–1972*, pp. 28, 29.

2. Mathews, *Osages,* p. 349.

3. John Joseph Mathews interview, August, 1974.

4. Ibid.; Jonathan Kwitny, *The Mullendore Murder Case,* p. 20.

5. Terry P. Wilson, *The Underground Reservation: Osage Oil,* pp. 30, 32; Orpha B. Russell, "Chief James Bigheart of the Osages," *Chronicles of Oklahoma,* Vol. 32, No. 4 (Winter, 1954–55): 388, 389.

6. W. S. Fitzpatrick, comp., *Treaties and Laws of the Osage Nation as Passed to November 26, 1890,* pp. 51–55.

7. Ibid., pp. 56, 57.

8. Russell, "Chief James Bigheart of the Osage," p. 389.

9. Ibid.; Wilson, *Underground Reservation,* pp. 34, 35.

10. Wilson, *Underground Reservation,* p. 100.

11. Mathews, *Osages,* p. 772; Baird, *Osage People,* pp. 67, 68; Garrick Alan Bailey, *Changes in Osage Social Organization 1673–1906,* p. 89.

12. Baird, *Osage People,* p. 68; Wilson, *Underground Reservation,* p. 34.

13. Mathews, *Osages,* pp. 772, 773; Baird, *Osage People,* pp. 70, 71; Russell, "Chief James Bigheart," p. 390; Wilson, *Underground Reservation,* p. 97.

14. The Osage rolls are the official tribal listing of members of the Osage tribe. Many non-Osages had also gotten on the Osage rolls during the tribal moves. In 1896 proof of Osage ancestry had to be established before a name was entered in the official Osage rolls at the Osage Agency in Pawhuska, Oklahoma. Muriel Wright, *A Guide to the Indian Tribes of Oklahoma,* p. 191; Wilson, *Underground Reservation,* p. 90.

15. Mathews, *Osages,* p. 773.

16. Mathews, *Osages,* p. 773; Wilson, *Underground Reservation,* p. 97.

17. Mathews, *Osages,* p. 772; Ralph A. Barney, *Laws Relating to the Osage Tribe of Indians from May 18, 1824, to March 2, 1929,* pp. 89, 90; Baird, *Osage People,* pp. 86, 88.

18. Barney, *Laws Relating to the Osage Tribe,* p. 44.

19. Barney, *Laws Relating to Osage Tribe,* p. 40; James Ballard, ed., *The World of the American Indians* (Washington, D.C.: National Geographic Society, 1974), p. 365; Kwitny, *Mullendore,* p. 21.

20. Wilson, *Underground Reservation,* pp. 127, 128.

21. Barney, *Laws Relating to the Osage Tribe,* p. 62.

22. John Collier, *The Indians of the Americas,* p. 244.

23. Mathews interview, August, 1974.

24. Kate Lester Jones, "Osage Indians," *Oklahoma Today,* Vol. 36, No. 3 (May–June, 1986): 32, 33.

25. Renard Strickland, *The Indians in Oklahoma,* pp. 70, 71.

Chapter 2. The History of the I'n-Lon-Schka

1. Rennard Strickland, *The Indians in Oklahoma,* p. 108.

2. Kate Lester Jones, "Osage Indians," *Oklahoma Today,* Vol. 36, No. 3 (May–June, 1986): 34.

3. Archie Mason, Jr., interview, August 5, 1987; Morris Lookout interview, August 4, 1987.

4. Morris Lookout interview, June 13, 1976; Archie Mason interview, June, 1976; Jones, "Osage Indians," p. 35; Ed Red Eagle interview, June, 1976.

5. Bruno Nettl, *An Introduction to Folk Music in the United States,* pp. 36, 37.

6. Terry P. Wilson, *The Underground Reservation: Osage Oil,* pp. 201, 202.

7. John Joseph Mathews, *The Osages: Children of the Middle Waters,* p. 781.

8. "Retired Teachers Hear Osage Historian," *Pawhuska Daily Journal-Capital,* March 14, 1975, p. 3.

9. The centennial of the Pawhuska I'n-Lon-Schka was celebrated in June of 1984; Ed Red Eagle interview, January, 1975.

10. Joseph C. Mason to Archie L. Mason, April 8, 1962.

11. Morris Lookout interview, August 4, 1975.

12. Clark Wissler, *General Discussion of Shamanistic and Dancing Societies,* pp. 859, 860; William K. Powers, *Indians of the Northern Plains,* p. 175.

13. Wissler, *Dancing Societies,* p. 861.

14. Ibid., pp. 871–73; Jones, "Osage Indians," p. 35.

15. Frances Densmore, *Teton Sioux Music,* p. 468.

16. Wissler, *Dancing Societies,* p. 862.

17. Densmore, *Teton Sioux Music,* pp. 468, 469.

18. Tony Isaacs, *War Dance Songs of the Poncas,* record, Taos, New Mexico, 1967. The purpose of this unusual reference is to illustrate the wide public usage of the term *war dance* today. The songs on the record are not from war dances. John Joseph Mathews interview, July 1974.

19. Archie Mason, Jr., interview, June 29, 1987.

20. Powers, *Indians of the Northern Plains,* p. 176.

21. Densmore, *Teton Sioux Music,* p. 472.

22. Ibid., pp. 469, 471.

23. Ibid., p. 472.

24. Ibid.

25. Ibid.

26. Maudie Cheshewella interview, July 7, 1987.

Chapter 3. Traditions of the I'n-Lon-Schka

1. John Joseph Mathews, *The Osages: Children of the Middle Waters,* p. 781. In later I'n-Lon-Schkas there was a slight change in the traditional order: Hominy held the I'n-Lon-Schka on the second week and Pawhuska on the third or fourth week.

Sometimes the name I'n-Lon-Schka is used by tribal members to refer to the ongoing committee structure as well as to the dances themselves. I will use the term only to refer to the ceremonial dances and will use the term *dance organization* to refer to the entire committee structure. I will use the term *dance committee* to refer to the small subgroup of the dance organization consisting of the Dance Chairman and his dance committee. The dance committee, Drumkeeper, Tail Dancers, and Whipmen are expected to dance in the I'n-Lon-Schka in all three villages. It is optional for other Osage dancers—those who have been introduced to the dance but who are not I'n-Lon-Schka dance committeemen or officials—to dance in all three I'n-Lon-Schkas.

2. "Tribal Ceremonial Dancing Begins Today in Grayhorse," *Fairfax Chief,* June 5, 1975, p. 1.

3. Class lecture, discussion with John Henry Mashunkashay, Baker University, January, 1984.

4. Archie L. Mason to the author, January 1975; Joseph C. Mason to Archie L. Mason, April 8, 1962.

5. Joseph C. Mason to Archie L. Mason, April 8, 1962.

6. A complete listing of the participants in the Grayhorse 1975 I'n-Lon-Schka dance organization is included in Appendix A.

7. Class lecture, discussion with John Henry Mashunkashay, Baker University, January, 1984.

8. Joseph C. Mason to Archie L. Mason, April 8, 1962. The I'n-Lon-Schka drum is never used for powwow dances (described in the preface), social dances, or handgames.

9. At the powwow, raffles and collections are a common occurrence and a part of this social occasion. As described in the preface, the powwows are a social event and do not have the set protocol or rules, committee structure, and set number of days that the ceremonial dances have.

10. The usual length of each of the dances within the I'n-Lon-Schka is approximately two hours. Each dance consists of a number of songs.

11. Often the advisors are asked to speak in behalf of women who are without older men in their families. At Hominy the women speak for themselves, but not at Grayhorse or Pawhuska.

12. The Tail Dance is the chorus of the previous song repeated, and it is usually a very short dance.

13. The coup stick (from the French *coup,* "stroke") is a symbol kept from the old warrior days. It is a small stick that was once used to touch an enemy. The touch was called "counting coup." This was considered a much braver feat than killing the enemy from a safe distance. The coup stick is still carried today as a part of the Osage men's traditional dress, even by those who have not earned the right to be a warrior.

The custom of only the host Head Tail Dancer's signaling for an encore is changing, as many Tail Dancers raised their coup sticks for repeats in some of the I'n-Lon-Schka dances I witnessed in the late 1970s and 1980s. However, in the 1974 Grayhorse I'n-Lon-Schka a Tail Dancer who raised his coup stick for a repeated chorus was fined because he was not the host Head Tail Dancer.

14. This tone is not a definite pitch but a resonant, deep tone that is considered the "right" tone by the drummers. They recognize immediately whether the drum has been properly prepared, as it will have a dull tone if it has not been heated thoroughly. In one of the 1976 I'n-Lon-Schka dances I heard a dull drum tone in an afternoon dance.

15. Morris Lookout interview, August 5, 1987.

16. Ibid.

17. Ibid.

18. This speech is on a tape from the 1976 Pawhuska I'n-Lon-Schka. Several young men were being given responsible positions in the singer-drummer circle, and this speech was to encourage them as well as to encourage those who had served over a longer period of time "around the drum."

19. Red Eagle interview, August, 1976.

20. The number of family songs sometimes extends this event into the evening. For example, during the Grayhorse family and individual song day in 1976, the dance began at 2:00 P.M. and was not finished until 7:30 P.M.

21. Archie Mason interview, July 7, 1987.

22. The opening prayers usually ask for God's blessing on the members of the tribe and on the I'n-Lon-Schka ceremonies.

23. From a tape of the 1976 Grayhorse I'n-Lon-Schka.

24. Ibid.

25. Mathews, *Osages,* p. 782.

26. Two young Ponca dancers seated in front of me at the 1976 Grayhorse family song day received money many times during the afternoon from members of different families whose family songs were sung.

27. The term *give-away days* is used by tribal members to refer to the days on which rations are given away, or to the family song day, in which many gifts are given throughout the dance.

28. From a tape of the 1976 Grayhorse Sunday afternoon I'n-Lon-Schka dance.

29. The singers are not usually in the traditional dress.

30. The entrance of the dancers is determined by the Dance Chairman and his interpretation of the rules of his village. This has changed in Grayhorse since I have been observing these dances.

31. I have seen women seated in the dance arena being asked to move by the Whipmen as the crowd of men dancers grew, forcing the need for all available bench space inside the dance arena for the men. The women withdrew to the bleachers outside the dance arena.

32. The acceptance-of-the-drum ceremony is sometimes referred to by tribal members as the "buying-" or "paying-for-the-drum" ceremony.

33. Ed Red Eagle interview, July 7, 1987.

34. Some of the shawls and blankets were decorated with Osage ribbon work, while others were the brightly striped Pendleton wool Indian

blankets. These blankets and shawls alone represent a sizable investment of money for the new Drumkeeper and his family, not including the expenses for the horse, Osage wedding dresses, and food for the guests. A more complete listing of these gifts is included in Appendix B.

35. Traditionally the Dance Chairman conducts the introduction-to-the-dance ceremony. However, in recent years, though Pawhuska and Hominy adhere to the old tradition, Grayhorse has allowed advisors, as well as the Dance Chairman, to conduct this ceremony. Archie L. Mason, former Grayhorse Dance Chairman and advisor in the 1970s and 1980s, conducted most of the introduction-to-the-dance ceremonies at the 1975 Grayhorse I'n-Lon-Schka.

36. From a tape of the 1976 Grayhorse I'n-Lon-Schka.

37. The old tradition was used for Francis Pipestem as he was introduced to the dance in the 1975 Grayhorse I'n-Lon-Schka.

38. Morris Lookout interview, August, 1975.

39. Kate Lester Jones, "Osage Indians," *Oklahoma Today,* Vol. 36, No. 3 (May–June, 1986): 35.

40. These fines vary in size according to the seriousness of the violation of rules and regulations. I have heard fines announced from five dollars to twenty-five dollars.

41. In later Grayhorse I'n-Lon-Schkas there was some change from the public fining and announcements I had observed in the 1974 and 1975 ceremonies. Fewer public announcements were made of the fines, and most persons losing articles on the dance floor went directly to the Whipmen to reclaim them.

42. Florence Rheam, "Osages Preserving Tribal Crafts," *Tulsa Sunday World,* June 10, 1973, p. 11.

Chapter 4. The I'n-Lon-Schka Music

1. Frances Densmore, *American Indians and Their Music,* p. 59.

2. Charles Hamm, Bruno Nettl, and Ronald Byrnside, *Contemporary Music and Music Cultures,* p. 114.

3. Densmore, *American Indians,* p. 128; William K. Powers, *Indians of the Northern Plains,* p. 116. I have recorded examples of the tremolo on the tape "Excerpts of Music from the Osage I'n-Lon-Schka," deposited in the Music Division, Bird Library, Syracuse University. Archie Mason, Jr., interview, August 5, 1987.

4. Densmore, *American Indians,* p. 128; Powers, *Indians of the Northern Plains,* p. 171.

5. Densmore, *American Indians,* pp. 102–103.

6. Arthur C. Edwards and W. Thomas Marrocco, *Music in the United States,* p. 69; Densmore, *American Indians,* p. 128.

7. Bruno Nettl, *An Introduction to Folk Music in the United States,* p. 35; Densmore, *American Indians,* p. 128.

8. Frederick R. Burton, *American Primitive Music,* pp. 89, 90.

9. Hamm, Nettl, and Byrnside, *Contemporary Music,* pp. 114, 117; Densmore, *American Indians,* p. 130.

10. Roberta Campbell Lawson, *Indian Music Programs,* p. 13; John Joseph Mathews interview, July, 1974.

11. Densmore, *American Indians,* p. 77.

12. Alice C. Fletcher, *Indian Story and Song from North America,* p. 12; Powers, *Indians of the Northern Plains,* pp. 167, 168; Densmore, *American Indians,* p. 31.

13. John Joseph Mathews interview, July, 1974; Archie Mason, Jr., interview, August 5, 1987.

14. The skips of perfect fourths and fifths occur as melodic motifs and phrases are repeated, either exactly or sequentially. See Musical Example 2, the Franklin Shaw Individual Song, between phrases *B* and *C.*

15. According to Lookout, the Osages belong to that large group of American Indians known as Southern Indians, and their drumming style is that of the Southern Indians. The Northern Indian drumming style does not have the light and heavy beats, but all of the same kind.

16. Francis La Flesche, *The Osage Tribe: Rite of the Chiefs; Sayings of the Ancient Men,* pp. 300, 301.

17. Powers, *Indians of the Northern Plains,* p. 171.

18. In the old days there would also be a closing song to which no one danced. That is no longer performed, and the dances simply stop when the Dance Chairman decides it is time.

19. Morris Lookout interview, June 14, 1976.

20. Ibid.

21. Ibid.

22. Morris Lookout interview, August, 1975.

23. I am certain there are other categories of which I am not aware, both in the past and in the 1970s and 1980s I'n-Lon-Schkas. I am dependent for this information on oral sources, and those listed are the ones that have been described to me.

24. Morris Lookout interview, August, 1975.

25. Morris Lookout interview, June, 1976.

26. Ibid.

27. Morris Lookout interview, June, 1977.

28. All of the individual songs described are available on tapes in the author's collection. The 1967 tapes are in a collection of John Joseph Mathews, who allowed me to make a copy of his tapes.

29. The tape "Excerpts of Music from the Osage I'n-Lon-Schka" is deposited in the Music Division, Bird Library, Syracuse University.

30. Morris Lookout interview, August, 1975.

Chapter 5. The I'n-Lon-Schka Dance

1. Kate Lester Jones, "Osage Indians," *Oklahoma Today,* Vol. 36, No. 3 (May–June, 1986): 35; Jamake Highwater, *Ritual of the Wind,* p. 140; Ed Red Eagle interview, July 7, 1987.

2. Ed Red Eagle interview, January, 1975.

3. The average length of an evening or afternoon dance is approximately one and one-half to two hours. In the 1977 Grayhorse I'n-Lon-Schka I heard Dance Chairman Browning Pipestem end the Saturday afternoon dances as the dancers were beginning to perform the faster style.

4. "Osage National Monument Proposed," *Pawhuska Daily Journal-Capital,* September 29, 1972, Sec. H., p. 1 (based on an interview with John Joseph Mathews).

5. Bernard S. Mason, *Dances and Stories of the American Indians,* p. 10.

6. Archie Mason interview, July 7, 1987.

7. Francis La Flesche, *The Osage Tribe: Rite of the Chiefs; Sayings of the Ancient Men,* pp. 66–116.

8. Mason, *Dances and Stories,* p. 15.

9. Ibid., pp. 18, 19.

10. Ibid., pp. 37, 38.

11. Ibid., pp. 20, 21.

Chapter 6. The Osage Traditional Dress

1. Florence Rheam, "Osages Preserving Tribal Customs," *Tulsa Sunday World,* June 10, 1973, Sec. H., p. 1.

2. Burnis Argo, "Osage Artists," *Oklahoma Today,* Vol. 36, No. 3 (May–June, 1986): 29. In my many visits to Pawhuska during the 1970s I have seen Georgeann Robinson, Maudie Cheshawalla, Ida Penn, and others working on finger-woven belts and garters and ribbon work on skirts and leggings for individual dancers in the I'n-Lon-Schka.

3. Archie Mason interview, January, 1975.

4. Georgeann Robinson died in 1985.

5. Georgeann Robinson interview, January, 1975.

6. Yvonne Litchfield, "The Osages May Have the Last of the Bartered Brides," *Tulsa Daily World,* August 20, 1970, p. 7.

7. John Joseph Mathews interview, July, 1974.

8. Osage wedding dresses were given by the new Drumkeeper at Grayhorse in June, 1975, to six Osage women being honored for their past work and support in the I'n-Lon-Schka dance organization. This occurrence is mentioned in chapter 3.

9. Linda Martin, "Naomi Wagoshe Revives Osage Ribbon Work," *Tulsa Daily World,* June 21, 1976, Sec. A, p. 8.

10. Archie Mason, Jr., interview, August 5, 1987.

11. Norman Feder, *American Indian Art,* pp. 13, 16, 18.

12. Ibid., p. 18; Martin, "Naomi Wagoshe," p. 8.

13. "Kansas City Museum Announces New Osage Exhibit," *Osage Nation News,* June, 1978, p. 2.

14. Georgeann Robinson interview, January, 1975.

15. Argo, "Osage Artists," p. 28; Alta R. Turner, *Finger Weaving: Indian Braiding,* p. 4.

16. Maudie Cheshewalla interview, January, 1975.

17. John Joseph Mathews interview, June, 1974.

18. Argo, "Osage Artists," p. 29.

19. Feder, *American Indian Art,* p. 26.

20. John Joseph Mathews interview, June, 1974.

21. Ibid.; "Osage National Monument Proposed," *Pawhuska Daily Journal-Capital,* September 29, 1972, Sec. H, p. 2. (A special centennial paper celebrating the Osage tribe's one hundred years in Pawhuska, Oklahoma.)

22. Terry P. Wilson, *The Underground Reservation: Osage Oil,* p. 200.

Chapter 7. New Ways for Old Traditions

1. John Joseph Mathews interview, July, 1974; Terry P. Wilson interview, September, 1987.

2. Ed Red Eagle, Jr., interview, August 16, 1987.

3. Archie Mason, Jr., interview, August 5, 1987; Ed Red Eagle, Jr., interview, August 16, 1987.

4. Archie Mason, Jr., interview, June 20, 1987.

5. Ed Red Eagle, Jr., interview, August 16, 1987.

6. Archie Mason, Jr., interview, June 20, 1987.

7. Ibid.

8. Kate Lester Jones, "Osage Indians," *Oklahoma Today,* Vol. 36, No. 3 (May–June, 1986): 35.

9. Archie Mason, Jr., interview, June 20, 1987.

10. Archie Mason, Jr., interview, June 20, 1987; Ed Red Eagle, Sr., interview, July 7, 1987; and Ed Red Eagle, Jr., interview, August 16, 1987.

11. Archie Mason, Jr., interview, June 20, 1987.

12. Jones, "Osage Indians," p. 36.

13. Ed Red Eagle, Jr., interview, August 16; Archie Mason, Jr., interview, June 20, 1987.

14. Class lecture with John Henry Mashunkashay, Baker University, January, 1984.

15. Ibid.

16. Morris Lookout interview, August 5, 1987.

17. Rennard Strickland, *The Indians in Oklahoma,* p. 104.

Chapter 8. Significance of the I'n-Lon-Schka

1. John Joseph Mathews, *Wah'Kon-Tah: The Osage and White Man's Road,* p. 19.

2. Tape of the 1976 Pawhuska I'n-Lon-Schka.

3. Archie Mason, Jr., interview, June 20, 1987.

4. Archie Mason interview; Ed Red Eagle interview, July 5, 1987.

5. Terry P. Wilson, *The Underground Reservation: Osage Oil,* p. 200; Kate Lester Jones, "Osage Indians," *Oklahoma Today,* Vol. 36, No. 3 (May–June, 1986): 33.

6. Pawhuska I'n-Lon-Schka notes, 1984.

7. 1987 Hominy and Pawhuska I'n-Lon-Schka notes.

Bibliography

Allen, Joseph W. *Cho O-Nee to High Iron: Neodesha, Kansas, from 1865 to 1886.* Fredonia: Midwestern Litho, 1962.

An-Gal-Na. "The Green Corn Festival." *Oklahoma Today,* Vol. 26, No. 2 (Spring, 1976), pp. 30–31.

Argo, Burnis. "Osage Artists." *Oklahoma Today,* Vol. 36, No. 3 (May–June, 1986), pp. 28–29.

Bailey, Garrick Alan. *Changes in Osage Social Organization, 1673–1906.* Anthropological Papers No. 5. Eugene: University of Oregon, 1973.

Baird, David. *The Osage People: Centennial Issue, 1872–1972.* Phoenix: Indian Tribal Series, 1972.

Barney, Ralph A. *Laws Relating to the Osage Tribe of Indians from May 18, 1824, to March 2, 1929.* Pawhuska: Osage Printery, 1929.

Barrett, S. M. *Shinkah, the Osage Indian.* Oklahoma City: Harlow Publishing Co., 1916.

Baughman, Robert W. *Kansas in Maps.* Topeka: Kansas State Historical Society, 1961.

"Beautiful Women." *Pawhuska Daily Journal-Capital,* February 12, 1926, p. 8.

Behymer, F. A. "The Fortune of John Stink." *Saint Louis Post-Dispatch,* December 15, 1940, p. 4.

Ballard, Jules B. (ed.). *The World of the American Indian.* Washington, D.C.: National Geographic Society, 1974.

Burton, Frederick R. *American Primitive Music.* New York: Moffat, Yard and Co., 1909.

Buttree, Julia N. *Rhythm of the Redman.* New York: A. S. Barnes and Co., 1930.

Casey, Frances. "Andrew Bernard Canville." Paper presented at Osage Mission Historical Society, fourth annual Mission Day, May 9, 1987.

Catlin, George. *Letters and Notes on the North American Indians, 1796–1872.* New York: W. W. Norton and Co., 1947.

Catlin's Indian Gallery. Tulsa: Thomas Gilcrease Institute of American History and Art, 1973.

Chapman, Berlin B. "Secret Instructions and Suggestions to the Cherokee Commission." *Chronicles of Oklahoma,* Vol. XXVI, No. 4 (Winter, 1948–49), p. 32.

Collier, John. *The Indians of the Americas.* New York: W. W. Norton and Co., 1947.

Cronyn, George W. (ed.). *American Indian Poetry: An Anthology of Songs and Chants.* New York: Ballantine Books, 1972.

Dendel, Esther Warner. *The Basic Book of Fingerweaving.* New York: Simon and Schuster, 1974.

Densmore, Frances. *American Indians and Their Music.* New York: The Woman's Press, 1926.

———. *Teton Sioux Music.* Bureau of American Ethnology Bulletin 61. Washington, D.C.: Government Printing Office, 1918.

Eastman, Charles A. *The Soul of the Indian.* Boston and New York: Houghton and Mifflin Co., 1911.

Edwards, Arthur C., and W. Thomas Marrocco. *Music in the United States.* Dubuque, Iowa: Wm. C. Brown Co., 1968.

Ewers, John C. *Artists of the Old West.* Enlarged edition. Garden City, N.J.: Doubleday and Co., 1973.

Feder, Norman. *American Indian Art.* New York: Harry N. Abrams, 1965.

Finney, T. M. *Pioneer Days with the Osage Indians.* Bartlesville, Okla.: T. M. Finney, 1925.

Fisher, James. "Proud Heart Beats in Violent Osage History." *Kansas City Times,* November 28, 1974, Sec. A, pp. 1, 7. Based on an interview with John Joseph Mathews.

Fitzpatrick, W. S. *Treaties and Laws of the Osage Nation as Passed to November 26, 1890.* Cedar Vale, Kans.: Commercial Press, 1890.

Fletcher, Alice C. *Indian Story and Song from North America.* Boston: Small, Maynard and Co., 1900.

Foreman, Grant. *Indians and Pioneers.* New Haven: Yale University Press, 1930.

Graves, W. W. *The Broken Treaty: A Story of the Osage Country.* Saint Paul, Kans.: The Journal, 1935.

———. *Early Jesuits at Osage Mission.* Saint Paul, Kans.: W. W. Graves, 1916.

———. *The Life and Letters of Father Schoenmakers, S.J.* Parsons, Kans.: Commercial Publishers, 1928.

Hamm, Charles; Bruno Nettl; and Ronald Byrnside. *Contemporary Music and Music Cultures.* Englewood Cliffs, N.J.: Prentice-Hall, 1975.

Haskall, Henry C. "The Men Who Came in Quest of Silver, Beaver and Gold." *Kansas City Star, Star Magazine,* July 4, 1976, p. 18.

Highwater, Jamake. *Ritual of the Wind.* Toronto: Methuen Publications, 1984.

Irving, Washington. *The Sketch Book.* New York: Mershon Co., 1819.

———. *A Tour on the Prairies.* Ed. John Francis McDermott. Norman: University of Oklahoma Press, 1973.

Isaacs, Tony. Record jacket of "War Dance Songs of the Poncas." Taos: Indian House 2002, 1967.

Jones, Kate Lester. "Osage Indians." *Oklahoma Today,* Vol. 36, No. 3 (May–June, 1986), pp. 32–36.

Josephy, Alvin M., Jr. (ed.). *The American Heritage Book of Indians.* New York: American Heritage Publishing Co., 1961.
———. *The Horizon History of Africa.* New York: American Heritage Publishing Co., 1971.
"Kansas City Museum Announces New Osage Exhibit." *Osage Nation News,* June, 1978, p. 2.
Kappler, Charles J. *Indian Affairs,* vol. II, *Laws and Treaties.* Washington, D.C.: Government Printing Office, 1904.
Kenton, Edna. *The Indians of North America.* Two vols. New York: Harcourt, Brace and Company, 1927.
Kwitny, Jonathan. *The Mullendore Murder Case.* New York: Farrar, Strauss, Giroux, 1974.
Labadie, George V. *A Statement Containing Data in Support of the Osage Tribe of Indians' Contention That the Present Federal Supervision of Their Affairs Should Continue to April 8, 1983, and as Long Thereafter as the Minerals Are Produced in Paying Quantities with the Osage Indians Paying for Said Supervision.* Pawhuska: Osage Tribal Council, February 15, 1954.
La Flesche, Francis. *A Dictionary of the Osage Language.* Washington, D.C.: Bureau of American Ethnology, 1932.
———. *The Osage Tribe: Rite of the Chiefs; Sayings of the Ancient Men.* Bureau of American Ethnology, Thirty-ninth Annual Report, 1917–18. Washington, D.C.: Government Printing Office, 1918.
———. *The Osage Tribe: Rite of the Wa-Yo-Be.* Bureau of American Ethnology, Forty-fifth Annual Report, 1930. Washington, D.C.: Government Printing Office, 1930.
———. *The Osage Tribe: Two Versions of the Rite of Child-Naming.* Bureau of American Ethnology, Forty-third Annual Report, 1928. Washington, D.C.: Government Printing Office, 1928.
Larkin, Moscelyne. "The Dance." *Nimrod,* Vol. 16, No. 2 (Spring–Summer, 1972), pp. 43–47.
Lawson, Roberta Campbell. *Indian Museum Programs.* Tulsa: Federated Music Club, 1926.
Linderman, Frank. *Out of the North.* Saint Paul, Kans.: Saint Paul Book Co., 1938.
Linquist, G. E. E. "Indian Treaty Making." *Chronicles of Oklahoma,* Vol. XXVI, No. 4 (Winter, 1948–49), pp. 443–48.
Litchfield, Yvonne. "The Osages May Have the Last of the Bartered Brides." *Tulsa Daily World,* August 20, 1970, p. 7.
———. "Paleface World of Fashion," *Tulsa Daily World,* November 16, 1975, p. 3.
Logsdon, Guy. "John Joseph Mathews—A Conversation." *Nimrod,* Vol. 16, No. 2 (Spring–Summer, 1972), pp. 70–89.
MacDonald, A. B. "Stoic Osages in Tears as They Part with the Man Who Counseled Them for Sixteen Years." *Kansas City Star,* January 17, 1931, p. 4.

160   Bibliography

Marquis, Arnold. *A Guide to America's Indians.* Norman: University of Oklahoma Press, 1957.

Martin, Linda. "Naomi Wagoshe Revives Osage Ribbon Work." *Tulsa Daily World,* June 21, 1976, Sec. A, p. 8.

Mason, Bernard S. *Dances and Stories of the American Indian.* New York: Ronald Press Co., 1944.

Mathews, John Joseph. *The Osages: Children of the Middle Waters.* Norman: University of Oklahoma Press, 1961.

————. *Talking to the Moon.* Chicago: University of Chicago Press, 1945.

————. *Wah'Kon-Tah, The Osage and the White Man's Road.* Norman: University of Oklahoma Press, 1932.

McAllester, David P. *Indian Music of the Southwest.* Colorado Springs: Taylor Museum, Colorado Springs Fine Arts Center, 1961.

McClain, Sam. *Authentic Osage Indian Roll Book, 1906.* Pawhuska: Sam McClain, 1957.

Momaday, N. Scott. *The Way to Rainy Mountain.* Albuquerque: University of New Mexico Press, 1969.

Morgan, Lewis Henry. *The Indian Journals, 1859–62.* Ed. Leslie A. White. Ann Arbor: University of Michigan Press, 1959.

Nettl, Bruno. *An Introduction to Folk Music in the United States.* Detroit: Wayne State University Press, 1960.

————. *Theory and Method in Ethnomusicology.* Glencoe, Ill.: Free Press, Division of Macmillan Co., 1964.

Newman, Tillie Karns. *Black Dog Trail.* Boston: Christopher Publishing House, 1957.

Osage Indians' Centennial Celebration, 1872–1972. Pawhuska (Okla.) *Daily Journal,* Capital Centennial Edition, September 29, 1972.

"Osage Indians Petition Nixon." *Daily Oklahoman,* May 22, 1970, p. 6.

Osage Indians' Semi-Centennial Celebration, 1907–1957. Pawhuska: Osage Agency campus, June 15, 1957.

"Osage National Monument Proposed." *Pawhuska Daily Journal-Capital,* September 29, Sec. H, pp. 1–2.

Owens, Marty. "Plains Indians' Straight Dance." *Baker Orange,* March 13, 1975, p. 2.

Patterson, Patrick. *Woolaroc Museum, KeMoHa.* Bartlesville, Okla.: Frank Phillips Foundation, 1965.

Pawhuska I'n-Lon-Schka Centennial Booklet, 1884–1984. Pawhuska: Osage Ceremonial Committee, June, 1984.

Powers, William K. *Indians of the Northern Plains.* New York: G. P. Putnam's Sons, 1969.

Prettyman, W. S., and Robert Cunningham. *Indian Territory.* Norman: University of Oklahoma Press, 1957.

"Retired Teachers Hear Osage Historian." *Pawhuska Daily Journal-Capital,* March 14, 1975, p. 3.

Rheam, Florence. "Osages Preserving Tribal Crafts." *Tulsa Sunday World,* June 10, 1973, Sec. H, pp. 1–3, 11.

Robinson, C. H. *Hawk the Young Osage.* Boston: L. C. Page and Co., 1928.
Russell, Orpha B. "Chief James Bigheart of the Osages." *Chronicles of Oklahoma,* Vol. XXXII, No. 4 (Winter, 1954–55), pp. 384–94.
Seymour, Warren. *The Indians Today.* New York: Benjamin H. Sanborn and Co., 1926.
Shirk, George H. "Peace on the Prairies." *Chronicles of Oklahoma,* Vol. XX-VIII, No. 1 (Spring, 1950), pp. 23–38.
"Six Indian Songs and Poems." Adapted by William Brandon from the original translations and commentaries. *Nimrod,* Vol. 16, No. 2 (Spring–Summer, 1972), pp. 5–11.
"St. Paul, Kansas." *Kansas Knight,* May, 1922, p. 4C.
Strickland, Rennard. *The Indians in Oklahoma.* Second ed. Norman: University of Oklahoma Press, 1981.
Tixier, Victor. *Travels on the Osage Prairies.* Ed. John Francis McDermott. Trans. Albert J. Salvan. Second ed. Norman: University of Oklahoma Press, 1968.
Tomkins, William. *Universal Indian Sign Language.* San Diego: William Tomkins, 1927.
"Tribal Ceremonial Dancing Begins Today in Grayhorse." *Fairfax Chief,* June 5, 1975, p. 1.
Turner, Alta R. *Finger Weaving: Indian Braiding.* Second ed. New York: Sterling Publishing Co., 1974.
Unrau, William. *The Kansa Indians: The History of the Wind People.* Norman: University of Oklahoma Press, 1971.
Veeder, Sal. "Interesting Facts of Oklahoma—The Osage." *Tulsa Daily World,* April 17, 1855, p. 3.
Verrill, A. Hyatt. *The American Indian.* New York: D. Appleton and Company, 1927.
Warner, Esther. *Fingerweaving.* New York: Simon and Schuster, 1974.
Wilson, Terry P. *The Underground Reservation: Osage Oil.* Lincoln and London: University of Nebraska Press, 1985.
Wissler, Clark. *General Discussion of Shamanistic and Dancing Societies.* Anthropological Papers of the American Museum of Natural History, Vol. XI. Washington, D.C.: Government Printing Office, 1916.
Wright, Muriel H. *A Guide to the Indian Tribes of Oklahoma.* Fifth ed. Norman: University of Oklahoma Press, 1971.
Zornow, William Frank. *Kansas: A History of the Jayhawk State.* Norman: University of Oklahoma Press, 1957.

Audio Materials

Cassette tapes in the author's collection.
1967, 1975, 1976, and 1977 Grayhorse I'n-Lon-Schka music
1974, 1975, 1976, and 1977 Pawhuska I'n-Lon-Schka music
1974 and 1976 Hominy I'n-Lon-Schka music

Osage language with Mabel Logan, January, 1975

Shaw Family Song, sung by Morris Lookout, August, 1975

Interviews with John Joseph Mathews, Ed Red Eagle, Morris Lookout, and John Shaw

"Excerpts of Music from the Osage I'n-Lon-Schka." Cassette tape recorded by Alice Anne Callahan, deposited at the Music Division, Bird Library, Syracuse University, New York.

Ponca War Songs. Two vols. Taos: Indian House 2001 and 2002, 1967. Recorded at Ponca City, Oklahoma.

Index

Acceptance of the drum: 49, 62–64, 151 n. 32; description of, at Grayhorse, 1975, 64–66; purpose of, 64; traditions of, 63–66

Advisors: 34–35, 43, 65; duties of, 43–44; spokesmen for women, 65–66, 150 n. 11

Allotment Act of 1906: communal property in, 15; mineral estate in, 14–15; for Osages, 13–17; see also allotment

American Indian dance, movements of: 103

American Indian music, characteristics of: 73–76

Bacon Rind: 19, 109, 138
Bantus, of Africa: 3–4
Bartlesville, Okla.: 10
Bear, Curtis Oren, as new Drumkeeper: 64–65
Bear, Jamison, family: 64–65
Big Beaver band: 11
Bigheart, James: at 1811 grand council, 11–12; opposes allotment, 13–14; and Osage constitution, 12
Big Horse, Andrew: 109
Beginning Song: analyzed, 79, 82–83, 88; as calling song, 90; compared to Franklin Shaw song, 79, 82; no dancing to, 91; tempo of, 85, 91; transcribed, 81; used at 1976 I'n-Lon-Schka

in Grayhorse, Hominy, and Pawhuska, 91; see also Calling Songs
Blackbird, Mr. (grandfather of Girard Fish): 56
Blackbird, John, Sr.: 25
Black Dog II: 13, 23
Blood quantum: 32
Bone whistles: 29, 77
Bowman, Barbara: 65
Bowman, King: 49; as "retiring" Grayhorse Drumkeeper, 64–65; see also Drumkeeper
Bradshaw, Scott: 134
"Buffalo-Pawing-Earth Moon, June": 33
Bureau of Indian Affairs, U.S.: 13

Cahill, Holger, and Osage Tribal Museum: 125–26
Calling songs: 90–91
Catholic Church: 15
Cedar-burning ceremony: at feast of the mourners, 61–62; at I'n-Lon-Schka, 54; tribal beliefs of, 53–54, 62
Cedarman: at Feast for the Mourners, 61–62; at I'n-Lon-Schka, 53–54; see also cedar-burning ceremony
Ceremonial dances: banning of American Indian, 4–5; basic steps of, 103; common characteristics of, 4, 97; men and women in, 98, 100; in tribal

Ceremonial dances (*continued*)
societies, 3–5; *see also* I'n-Lon-
Schka; powwows
Cherokees: 9, 14
Cheshewalla, Maudie: 108–109,
120, 122–23, 154 n. 2; as au-
thority on finger weaving,
123–24
Chiefs' Society: 26
Claremore (Osage chief): 12
Clark, Jim: 50
Closing song: 153 n. 18
Collier, John: 17, 126
Competency of Osages, certifi-
cate of: 16, 147 n. 1
Conklin, Roscoe: 50
Conscious composition: 76
Cooks: 35, 44, 51; as host cooks,
59; importance of, 139; individ-
ual song of, 43; *see also* Cooks
Song
Cooks Song: 93
Coups: 75, 131; stick, 31, 44, 70,
118, 150 n. 13
Crow belt: 26; *see also* I-Ru-Shka;
Omaha Grass Dance

Dakota dance ceremony: 27
Dance arbors: 29, 41, 44, 52–53,
64–65; cedar burning in, 54;
description of, 53; spectator
seating at, 53; *see also*
Roundhouse
Dance ceremonies: *see* ceremonial dances
Dance Chairman (Head Com-
mitteeman): 24, 33, 37–38,
40–41, 43–44, 46–49, 51, 55,
134; Browning Pipestem as, 21,
51, 56, 65; death of, 53; duties
of, 38, 40, 62–63, 66, 69–70,
72, 88, 151 n. 30, 152 n. 35,
153 n. 18; Ed Red Eagle as,
49–50, 52, 55, 65; host, 49–50,
52, 55, 57, 69; importance of,
38, 40; individual song of, 93;

new, 64–65; pressures on
1970s and 1980s Dance
Chairmen, 128–29; announce
gifts, 56; seating of, 58; song
of, 93; symbolism of red
feather of, 118; visiting, 55
Dance committee: 33–35, 40–41,
49, 58, 62–63, 150 n. 1; admittance and seating of, 57–58;
importance of, 40–41; rank of, 40
Dance organization: 19, 33–35,
37–38, 40–41, 43–45, 51,
149–50 n. 1; admittance and
seating of, 57; appointment of,
37; choosing of family songs
by, 92–93; gifts to former
members of, 64–65; meetings
of, 38, 40; posititons of, 34–35;
problems of large dance organization, 128; rules established,
34, 72; *see also* Advisors;
Cooks; Dance Chairman;
Drumkeeper; Singer-Drum-
mers; Singers; Tail Dancers;
Whipmen
Dancers, men: 41, 43, 46; body
positions of, 100, 107; dance
steps and movements of,
98–100, 103–105, 107; direction around drum, 99; education of young dancers, 129–31;
gentes represented in, 99; increase in number of, 127–28;
respect for drum, 52; seating
of, 58; teaching dances to,
98–99
Dancers, women: 58, 98, 100,
127, 151 n. 31
Dance sets: 55, 85; flow of music
and dance in, 99; makeup
of, 88
Dance steps: 97, 99; crossed toe-
heel, 103–104; flat-foot, 105;
flat-heel, 104; heel-toe, 104;
toe-heel, 103–104; trot,
105–106; variation in, 107

Dawes and Curtis acts of Congress: 13
Department of the Interior, U.S.: 5, 13
Dhegiha Sioux: 22–23, 33
Dinners: at Grass Dance, 31–32; importance of, 31–32, 59–60; at I'n-Lon-Schka, 59–60; for I'n-Lon-Schka dance organization, 38, 60–61; for mourners, 44, 53, 61–62; *see also* Cooks; Drumkeeper
Drum: expressions about, 52, 92–93; importance of in I'n-Lon-Schka, 19, 21–22, 32, 37, 49, 51; materials of, 45, 74, 77; as musical instrument, 77; ownership of, 52; position of, in dance arbor, 46; preparation of, 45–46, 77; protection of, 37, 52, 150 n. 8; respect for, 40, 52, 107; when placed in dance arbor, 52
Drumbeats: cues for, 84; description of, 84, 153 n. 15; patterns of, 84–85; for Warrior and War songs, 85–86
Drumkeeper: 19, 25, 31–34, 37–38, 43, 47, 49, 51–52; age of, 19, 35; choice of traditions, 72; Curtis Oren Bear as new, 64–66; death of, 44, 53; duties of, 37–38, 52, 60–61, 66, 91; expenses of, 37, 134, 144, 151 n. 34; host, 55, 57–58; King Bowman as former, 65; length of tenure as, 62; Osage pride in children reflected in position of, 136; present-day pressures on, 128–29; receiving gifts, 56; selection of new, 62–63; training of, 35, 37; visiting, 55; *see also* Drumkeeper's Song
Drumkeeper's Song: 93
Drummers: *see* Singers-Drummers (men)

Drum Warmer: 29, 35, 45, 52; appointment of, 45; duties of, 45, 57, 63, 151 n. 14
Dwellers upon the Hilltop: 7
Dwellers in the Thorny Thicket: 7
Dwellers in the Upland Forest: 7

Eagle, Wilkie: 50
Eldest, importance of: 19

Family song day: 43; length of, 150 n. 20; program and number of songs on, 93; traditions of, 56–57, 91
Family Songs (individual): 49; analysis of melodies of family songs, 79, 82–83; belong to, 91; in honor of, 56, 76, 91; in I'n-Lon-Schka, 92–93; new on drum in 1976 Grayhorse I'n-Lon-Schka, 94; removing from drum, 93; text of, 92; those on drum in both the 1967 and 1976 Grayhorse I'n-Lon-Schkas, 93–94; traditions of, 56, 76, 91; when sung, 56, 91; *see also* Franklin Shaw, Hunk-A-Hoppy, Thomas Joe Lane individual songs
Fancy dance: *see* powwows
Feast for the Mourners: 44, 53, 61–62
Fines: 31–32, 41, 43, 152 n. 40, 69–70
Finger weaving: description of, 122; favorite Osage designs in, 122–23; history of, 122; importance of, to traditional dress, 108–109, 120; materials, 122; as religious art, 120; spider motif in, 123; time to produce, 123
Fish, Girard: 56
Fletcher, Alice: 26, 87
Flutes, wooden or bone: 74, 76–77
Foster, Henry: 13

Franklin Shaw Individual Song: analyzed, 79; compared to Beginning Song, 79, 82; composition of, 88; on drum in 1976 Grayhorse I'n-Lon-Schka, 95; text and translation of, 95; transcribed, 80; typical as American Indian song, 79, 82

Freeman, H. B.: 13

Full-Bloods: 12–14; see also Osage tribal council; Osage tribal elections

Gas, natural: 11
Gavin, Father (Catholic priest): 56
Geller, Todros: 126
Gentes: 99
Ghost Dance: 5
Gifts: 51; from absent members, 55; at acceptance of the drum, 64–66; on family-song and "giveaway" days, 56; by the honored, 31; at introduction to the dance, 69; at 1976 Grayhorse I'n-Lon-Schka, 151n. 26, 27, 151n. 34; for services performed, 70; see also "giveaways"
"Giveaways": 31, 43, 151n. 27
"Going-down": 100, 107; see also dancers (men)
Governor Joe (Paw-ne-no-pashe): 12
Grayhorse, Okla., and I'n-Lon-Schka at: 7, 15, 18–21, 33, 41, 43, 49, 55–56, 129–31, 152n. 35, 152n. 41; acceptance of drum in, 64–66; Beginning Song at, 91; Cedarmen in, 54; community organizations, 56; cooks' recognition at, 139; dances to open at, 71; dress, traditional motifs of, 118; dressing at, preparations, 111; Drum Keeper selected at, 62; drum placement at, 52, 57, 71;

drum received at, 7, 24–25; entrance and seating of dancers at, 57; family song day at, 93; fines at, 69–70; gifts at, 55–56, 151n. 34; individual and family songs at, 93–96; introduction to the dance in, 65–66; as Osage village, 7, 15, 129–31; raffles for, 38, 71; smoker at, 51; Town Crier selection, 50–51; tremolo at, 74; water boys at, 71; women in dance organization at, 60; see also I'n-Lon-Schka
Grayhorse district: see Grayhorse, Okla., I'n-Lon-Schka at
Grazing land, leasing of: 11, 13
Great, or Guardian, spirit: 3, 21, 76–77, 91
Great Lakes tribes, received technique of ribbon work: 119
Guardians: 17; see also competency

Head Cook: 34–35, 44
Head Singer-Drummer: 4, 25, 29, 35, 40, 52, 66; appointed by, 46; duties of, 46–49, 78, 84, 86, 90; honored as, 49, 56; importance of, 46, 49–50; Morris Lookout as, 4, 25, 47, 49–50; position in Singers' Circle, 46–48
Head Tail Dancer: 30–31, 46, 150n. 13; duties of, 44, 78
He-Tho-Shka (Ponca), He-Thu-Shka (Omaha): 28, 32
Highwater, Jamake: 97
Ho'Kah: 89
Hominy, Okla., and I'n-Lon-Schka at: 15, 18–19, 33, 41, 152n. 35; admittance and seating of dancers in, 57; Beginning Song at, 91; dress, traditional motifs in, 118; drum

received at, 7, 24–25; introduction to the dance at, 71; as Osage village, 7, 15, 130–131; raffles for I'n-Lon-Schka in, 38, 72; Town Crier selection in, 51; women in Dance organization in, 60; *see also* I'n-Lon-Schka

Howard, James H.: 22

Hunk-A-Hoppy Family Song: analysis of excerpt, 82, 83; one of first on Grayhorse drum, 94

I'n-lon: 19

I'n-Lon-Schka: ancestry of, 7, 22–27, 88; beliefs and importance of, 5, 17–21, 135; camps at, 58–59; cedar-burning at, 54; ceremonial dance style and steps in, 97–98, 103–105, 107; changes in dance in 1970s and 1980s, 133–34, 150 n. 13; characteristics of men's dancing in, 97–100, 103, 107; characteristics of women's dancing in, 100; dance organization of, 33–34; dance sets in, 88; dancers, men and women, 98, 100, 127; days of week of, 55–56; differences between village traditions of, 33, 38, 52, 54–55, 57, 60, 62–63, 69–72, 150 n. 22, 152 n. 35; direction of dancers in, 99; dressing and assembling of traditional dress in, 111–112; drum in, 19, 21–22, 32, 37, 49, 52; drumbeats in, 83–85; expense of, 37, 144; honoring of individuals at, 19, 55–56; importance of, in 1970s and 1980s, 136; individual ceremonies of, 40, 49, 62–69; interaction of music, dance and traditional dress in, 136–137; interruption of, 44, 53; leaders in 1970s and 1980s, 131, 133; learning of dances, 98–100;

length of individual dances in, 150 n. 10, 154 n. 3; meals of, 59–60, 139; meaning of term, 19; melodic rhythms of Osage songs in, 86–87; musical instruments in, 77; music tempos in, 85–86; and Omaha Grass Dance, 27–32; Osage bridal dress in, 115; Osage economic independence and, 98; Osage traditional dress in, 57, 108–109, 112; seating order at, 57–58; settings for, 7, 15, 44; signal bells at, 57, 111; songs of, 78–83; teaching of meaning and traditions of, 129–131; Wah'Kon-Tah in, time of year of, 19, 33, 53; village traditions of, 33, 38, 52, 54; vocal music characteristics in, 76–77; Wah'kon-Tah, 135–36; as Warrior Society, 131; as way of life, 137; women's roles in 1970s and 1980s, 138–139; women's traditional dress in, 112–113; *see also* acceptance of the drum; Grayhorse, Okla.; Hominy, Okla.; introduction to the dance; passing of the drum; Pawhuska, Okla.

Ickes, Harold, and Osage Tribal Museum: 125–126

Indian Territory: 7, 9–11, 18, 22, 24

Introduction to the dance: 44, 62; age of, 66; family choice of traditions, 69; gifts given at, 69; in Grayhorse, 1976, 68; purpose of, 66, 136; traditions of, 66, 68–69, 152 n. 37

I-Ru-Shka, Pawnee ceremony: 25–28

Jefferson, Thomas: 8, 116

Kansa: *see* Kaws

Kansas: 7, 9–10, 13–14, 18, 24

Kansas City Museum: 119
Kaw Indians: 7, 22–25, 27, 50,
    61, 88
Kemble, Chick and Jim: 50
Kidd, Darnell: 55
Kirk, Charles: 51, 94; as
    Grayhorse Smoker, 51–52
Kirk, Wilson, individual song of:
    94
Knee bells: 74, 77–78

Labadie, George: 125
Lady Singers' Song: 93
Lead singer: 48–49, 78, 84
Little Cook, Oliver: 50
Little Star, Eva, skirt of: 113, 115
Logan, Leroy: 138
Lookout, Fred: 95, 138
Lookout, Morris: 4, 20–21, 25,
    47, 49–50, 65, 88, 92, 153n. 15
Louisiana Purchase: 7–8, 116
"Lulu": see tremolo

Mashburn, Ted: 51
Mashunkashay, Ben, as Paw-
    huska's first Drumkeeper: 19
Mashunkashay, John Henry: 19,
    34; as Pawhuska Drumkeeper,
    35, 37
Mason, Archie: 21, 99; as cedar-
    man, 54; as Dance Chairman,
    94; dress decorations of, 109;
    individual song of, 94; at intro-
    duction to the dance, 68; on
    peyote religion and I'n-Lon-
    Schka, 138; redesigning of ot-
    ter, 112; see also cedarman
Mason, Archie, Jr.: 20–21, 27, 97,
    130–31, 133, 136
Mason, Joseph C.: 25, 34, 37; in-
    dividual song of, 94
Mathews, John Joseph: 17, 22, 33,
    56, 78; as grant author of oil
    paintings of Osage leaders,
    126; as sponsor of Osage Tribal
    Museum, 125–126; on song

composition, 75–76;
    Wah'Kon-Tah described by,
    135
Matin, Helen Pratt: 54
Mescalero Apache: 18
Miles, Laban J.: 13–14, 19
Mixed-bloods: 12–14; see also Os-
    age tribal council; Osage tribal
    elections

Nadel, Siegrid: 3
Native American Church: see
    peyote
Ne-Kah-he-pon-ah (Osage): 12
Northern Plains tribes: 25
Not Afraid, Mrs. (Crow): 55

Oil: 11; leasing of lands for, 13
Oklahoma, state and territory of:
    7, 9, 15, 17, 22; regional Indian
    craft style in, 119
Omaha Grass Dance: 25–27;
    comparison of I'n-Lon-Schka
    with, 27–32; see also He-Thu-
    Shka
Omaha Indians: 26
Oral sources: 98–99
Oral tradition: 21, 33–34, 50, 73,
    90, 128, 130
Osage Agency: 52
Osage bands: 55; see also
    Hominy, Okla; Grayhorse,
    Okla.; Pawhuska, Okla.
Osage beadwork: 112, 115,
    124–125
Osage braid; see finger weaving
Osage "brides", at I'n-Lon-
    Schka: 64–65
Osage County: 10, 15, 18
Osage headrights: 16–17
"Osage Indian village(s)" (com-
    munal property): 15, 21
Osage mourning ceremony: 90
Osage Nation: 12, 15, 52
Osage National Council: 12–13
"Osage Reign of Terror": 17

Osage reservation in Oklahoma:
10–11, 13
Osage traditional dress: adaptation of early twentieth-century
skirt, 113, 115; assembling of
men's, 111–112; assembling of
women's, 113–15; finger weaving, ribbon work, and beadwork as part of, 108–9, 115,
118, 120, 122, 124; handing
down of, 108–109; importance
of in I'n-Lon-Schka for men
and women, 57, 108; knee bells
in men's, 78; length of time to
create, 109; origin of designs,
crafts, materials in, 118–119;
present materials in, 109, 111,
113, 115; reflection of family
and individual in, 109; separate
pieces of men's, 109, 111; separate pieces of women's, 112–13;
symbolism of colors, motifs
and pieces of, 112, 116, 118;
value of, 108; *see also* finger
weaving; ribbon work
Osage treaties: 8
Osage tribal council: 15–16, 52;
business committee form of,
16; competency question,
16–17; *see also* Allotment Act
of 1906; Osage Tribal politics
Osage tribal elections: 12, 16
Osage tribal government: 11–12;
and allotment, 14–15; *see also*
Osage Nation; Osage National
Council; Osage tribal council
Osage Tribal Museum: 108, 123,
125–26
Osage tribal politics: 11–17; allotment, 13–16; factions in, 12–14
Osage tribal rolls: 14–15, 148 n.
14; *see also* allotment; Allot-
ment Act of 1906
Osage tribal trust: 10
Osage villages: *see* Allotment Act
of 1906; Grayhorse, Okla.;

Hominy, Okla.; Pawhuska,
Okla.
Osage war veterans: 131
Osage wedding dress: 64–65; de-
scription of, 115–16; as gifts at
I'n-Lon-Schka, 154 n. 8; history
of, 115–16
Otoe Indians: 61

Pah-Hu-Skah (White Hair) (early
nineteenth-century Osage
chief): 9
Pah-Hu-Skah (White Hair) (later
nineteenth-century Osage
chief): 10
Pan-Indianism: 22, 23; in Oklahoma Indian crafts, 119
Passing of the drum: 40, 62–63;
completed, 66; traditions in
Grayhorse of, 62; traditions in
Pawhuska of, 62–63; *see also*
I'n-Lon-Schka
Pawhuska, Okla., and I'n-Lon-
Schka at: 15, 18–19, 21, 33, 43,
49, 152 n. 35; admittance and
seating of dancers, 57; Beginning Song at, 91; cedarmen,
54; cooks, recognition of, 139;
dress, traditional motifs of,
118; drum, authority over, 51;
drum, placement of, 52, 57, 71;
drum, received in, 7, 24–25;
Drumkeeper, selection of, 62;
fines at, 70; head committeeman at, 72; introduction to
the dance in, 71; opening of
dances at, 71; as Osage capital,
10; as Osage County seat, 15;
as Osage village, 7, 130–31;
Osage Tribal Museum in, 108,
123; raffles at, 38, 72; Town
Crier, selection of, 51; Water
Boys at, 71; women in dance
organization at, 60; *see also* I'n-
Lon-Schka
Pawnee ceremony: *see* I-ru-Shka

Pawnee Indians: 25–26, 61, 75, 77
Penn, Ida: 154 n. 2
Petseemoah: 125
Peyote: 18; coming to Osages, 138; relation to I'n-Lon-Schka, 138
Pipestem, Browning: 21, 51; as host Dance Chairman, 56; as new Dance Chairman, 65, 94, 131, 139, 154 n. 3; *see also* Dance Chairman
Pipestem, Francis (Otoe), individual song of: 94
Pipestem, Francis, Jr.: 21
Pipestem, Rose: 65, 94
Pipestem, Wilson Kirk: 21
"Place on the drum," to: 55
Ponca City, Okla.: 10
Ponca Indians: 7, 22–25, 27–28, 50, 61, 88; language of, 89; *see also* I'n-Lon-Schka
Powers, William K.: 88
Powwows: 4, 38, 150 n. 8, 150 n. 9; audiences at, 97; dancing style of, 97–98; Osage Nation powwow, 52
Prairie Indians: 22, 25, 31; ribbon work coming to, 119, 124
Prairie Indians Grass Dance: *see* Omaha Grass Dance
Prairie Parkway (Okla.): 20
Prayer songs: 91
Protestant churches: 15

Quaker meeting house: 29; *see also* Dance Arbors

Raffles (lotteries): 38, 150 n. 9
Rations: 37, 43–44, 57; when given, 55
Rattles: 74, 78
Red Eagle, Ed: 21–22, 24, 97, 131, 133; as host Dance Chairman, 49–50, 52; as Pawhuska Dance Chairman, 49–50, 52, 55, 136; as visiting Dance Chairman, 55; on the peyote religion and I'n-Lon-Schka, 138; speaks on behalf of Rose Pipestem, 65; speeches by, 49–50, 55; *see also* Dance Chairman
Red Eagle, Ed, Jr.: 131
Rheam, Florence: 72
Rhythm: drum rhythms, 83; melodic rhythms, 86–87; *see also* drumbeats
Ribbon work: description of as Osage craft, 119; favorite Osage designs in, 119–20; history of, 119; importance of to Osage traditional dress, 108–9; symbolism of motifs and colors in, 118–19
Roach headdress: 25, 28; description of, 112; at introduction to the dance, 68; symbol of eagle feather in, 68–69; *see also* I-Ru-Shka; Omaha Grass Dance
Robinson, Georgeann: 154 n. 2; adaptation of older skirt, 113, 115; describes assembling and dressing in women's traditional dress, 113
Roundhouse: 29

Saucy Chief (Osage): 12–13
Schka: 19
Shaw, Cora, and family: 51, 55
Shaw, Franklin: as assistant chief and acting chief, 95; individual song of, 79–80, 82, 88, 95
Shaw, Jerry: 131; family of, 21
Shaw, John (son of Franklin): 66, 88, 95
Shaw, John (son of Jerry), as Grayhorse Drumkeeper: 131
Singers (women): 46, 151 n. 29; chosen by, 48; duties of, 48; individual song of, 93; seating of, 57, 73; singing of, 76
Singers-Drummers (men): 21, 35,

46, 49, 52, 88; abilities of, 75; chosen by, 48; drumbeats of, 76–77; drumsticks of, 77; dress, traditional, of, 151 n. 29; duties of, 48–49; honored, 49; importance of, 49–50, 75; numbers of, 76–77; seating of, 57, 75; singing of, 74, 76–77
Skiatook, Okla.: 56
Smoke Dance: 56
Smoker: 34; duties of, 51–52
Smoker song: 51
Songs: analysis of melodies, 78–79, 82–83, 153 n. 14; analysis of rhythms of melodies, 86–87; categories of, 49, 89, 153 n. 23; as "classics," 90; composition of, 88–89; Head Singer introduces, 46; importance of, 88, 90; learned by oral tradition, 90; "on the drum," 52; order of, 46, 89; ownership of, 88; strophic melodies, 89; texts and translations of, 89, 92, 137–38; *see also* Calling Songs; Family Songs; prayer songs; Smoker songs; Warrior and War songs
Sroufe, Gertrude: 49, 51, 65, 94–95
"Straight dance": *see* ceremonial dances
Strike Axe (Osage): 12
Stock, Gregg F.: 119
Sun Dance: 5

Tail Dance: 31, 84, 150 n. 12
Tail Dancers: 34–35, 84; importance of, 31, 44; respect for drum, 52
Tallchief, Mr. and Mrs. Harry: 68
Tallchief, Henry, individual song of: 95
Tallchief, John: 20, 68
Tempo: 85–86
Thomas Joe Lane Individual

Song: analysis of excerpt, 83; as new individual song, 93, 95–96
Town Crier: 29, 31, 35, 46; duties of, 50, 57, 62–63; gifts to, 70; importance of, 50; installation of Isaac Williams, 50–51
Tremolo: 73–74, 96
Tribal police: 38
Trot songs: 78, 87; dance step of, 105; from an old Osage mourning ceremony, 90
Tucker, Cody: 56
Tulsa, Okla.: 10, 131
Tyndall, Raymond: 51; *see also* Town Crier

Unconscious composition: 76
United States government: 7, 12, 16
Ursula, Sister (Catholic nun): 56

Vaux, George, Jr.,: 17
Vietnam: 131
Vocables: 21, 76, 89

Wah'Kon'Tah: 20–21, 50, 77, 135
Wah Sha'She (the Osage people): 49
Wah'We-See Individual Song: 92
Wakon Iron, Mr.: 88, 95
Waller, Marguerite: 23
War dance: 28
Warrior and War songs: 85–86, 91
Water Boys: 34–35, 37; duties of, 46; gifts to, 70; traditions of "watering," 46, 71
Watson, Mike: individual song of, 94; in Grayhorse and Pawhuska dance organizations, 94
Whipmen, 31, 34–35, 38, 55; dance clockwise around drum, 99; duties of, 41, 43, 46, 58, 61–63, 103; individual song of, 93; as host, 57–58, 70; receiving gifts, honor, 56

Whipmen's Song: 93
Whips: 38, 41
Whoops, as expression of men's
    gratitude: 73–74
Williams, Isaac: 21, 50–51; *see
    also* Town Crier
Williams, Johnny: 56–57; indi-
    vidual song of, 93; mother of,
    56, 94

Wilson, Terry: 127
Wissler, Clark: 25, 27
Woodland Indian ribbon work, 120
Wool broadcloth: 115
Works Progress Administration
    (WPA): 125
World Wars: 131

Yankton Sioux: 28